From Teacher To Tarot Reader

My Journey From Mainstream Teaching to Professional Tarot Reading

Becky Clarke

From Teacher To Tarot Reader
ISBN: 9798520529231

First published in Great Britain
in 2021 through Amazon
self-publishing service

Copyright © for this book is
owned by Becky Lisa Clarke

The author has asserted their right under the
Copyright, Design and Patents Act 1988
to be identified as the author of this work.
Disclaimer: real names/places
have been changed to protect the identities.

This book is sold subject to the condition that it
shall not, by way of trade or otherwise, be lent,
resold, hired out, or otherwise circulated without
the author's prior consent in any form of binding
or cover and without a similar condition, including
this condition, being imposed on the subsequent
publisher.

Produced by missdigitalmedia.co.uk

Dedication

This book is dedicated to my
ever supportive husband.

Contents

Author Bio	7
Part 1	**9**
Chapter 1: Past – Justice	11
Chapter 2: Present – Four Of Wands	28
Chapter 3: Challenges – Two Of Pentacles	36
Chapter 4: Mind – Ace of Swords	43
Chapter 5: Heart – Ace Of Cup	48
Chapter 6: Body – Eight Of Pentacles	52
Chapter 7: Soul – The High Priestess	59
Chapter 8: Potential Future – The World	64
Part 2	**73**
Chapter 9: Major Arcana	75
Chapter 10: Minor Arcana	77
Chapter 11: The Court Cards	82
Chapter 12: Tarot and Astrology Signs	84
Chapter 13: Key To Tarot Symbols	92
Chapter 14: To Infinity and Beyond!	97
Chapter 15: Numerology in Tarot	100
Chapter 16: The Fool's Journey	104
Chapter 17: Smoke Cleansing	106
Chapter 18: Tarot Myths	109
Chapter 19: The Good Guys	113
Chapter 20: The Scary Cards	116

Chapter 21: The Questions We All Want Answered	119
Chapter 22: Tarot for Your Year Ahead	124
Chapter 23: Colours in Tarot	129
Chapter 24: Shuffling the Cards	135
Chapter 25: Reversals	137
Chapter 26: Conducting a Reading	139
Chapter 27: Asking Good Questions	142
Chapter 28: Combining Cards	143
Chapter 29: Spread Suggestions	146
And Finally...	153
To Contact The Author	154

Author Bio

Photo courtesy of Kirsty Hardiman Photography.

Becky Clarke is a professional tarot reader and astrologer based in North Dorset in the UK. She is the creator of the online course *'Cracking The Astrology Code – Understanding Your Birth Chart For Beginners'* and has a BA(hons) Degree in teaching. This is her first book. When Becky isn't working in the spiritual realm, she can be found doing yoga in her garden, playing her oboe or paddle boarding around the Dorset coast.

Part 1

"You must really have some stories!"

I'd heard it said to me many times by many friends and they're not wrong. I'm in no way a seasoned pro in this job yet but already, in my first year as a professional tarot reader, I've heard many a tale of love, loss and everything in-between - but of course, due to ethical reasons and confidentiality, none of these tales have, or will ever, truly come to light. Although, wasting such valuable insight seems a missed opportunity when sharing all that I now understand and have learnt from the past year so I'm writing the book I'd like to have read twelve months ago.

To all of my wonderful clients, you are extremely unlikely to ever recognise yourself in this book. Your support and loyalty will always come first and will not be compromised in the following chapters.

CHAPTER ONE

Past - Justice

I'm a Libran through and through. For anyone who dabbles in astrology, my Sun, Saturn, Jupiter, Pluto and Rising sign are all Libra. With Justice being the tarot card for Libra, there is nothing else this chapter could have been named and boy, how the theme of justice runs through my life.

Born in Shoreham-By-Sea in the early 1980's, I was the first-born daughter of a bank manager and secretary, although my mum soon left that role when I was born, returning to different jobs later in life after my brother was born. I grew up in a pretty suburban area with tree-lined roads. I can remember the abundance of autumn leaves on the walk to and from Shoreham First School and how much I loved walking through them, my little brother still in the buggy.

Nothing in those early years ever indicated I'd end up working with tarot and later, astrology. In fact, I was pretty scared of the dark and usually went to sleep with my He-Man cassettes playing in the background to keep me company. As far as I know, although I've not looked back that far, there's no history of tarot readers, witches or similar in my family on either mum's or dad's side. Yet, despite my relatively *'normal'* upbringing, my interest in all things spiritual continued to grow with my age.

I used to love crackers at Christmas dinner. I couldn't wait to pull them and we were often ready, crackers in hand, before my mum even sat down on Christmas day. The main goal for me was to find the fortune telling fish that was usually made from some kind of plastic film that curled and twisted on your palm, often flipping right over to reveal your destiny. For younger readers who didn't experience the joy of the fortune telling fish, you had to watch closely at how the fish curled up or flipped in order to ascertain what your true destiny would be. As a child I was fascinated with them and they'd often hang around in our house long after the Christmas holidays. I believe you could also ask them questions, with the fish's final positioning revealing your answer. I suspect there were many plastic fish interrogated by me during the late 1980's, the poor things.

When I was around eight years old, we moved house and this is where the fun really started! We moved into a 1960's house that had been built on land that was used as a make-shift First World War hospital. I can remember when we moved in there were cannon balls in the garage, which my brother - then around five - and I, thought were really cool. We later found out that an admiral had first owned the property so they may well have been there from his time. That wasn't the only thing in the garage: I can still clearly picture, above a door that led into the house, an upside-down horseshoe nailed to the door frame. Traditionally horseshoes are considered lucky and hung up to catch good luck. Hung upside down however, they are known for letting all the luck flow out. It was promptly removed by my dad and certainly no harm came to any of us in the house but it does stick in my memory, as perhaps the start of some of the quirks that were to come in that house.

I got the larger of the bedrooms available to my brother and me. I can remember being really wowed by it, as it felt much bigger than my last bedroom and had an old sink in it. It's funny what sticks in the memory. I never used it and it was soon removed to make-way for a desk to do my homework on... this is where my bedroom became very interesting! Whether there had always been some kind of strange energy in that room and I just can't remember it, or whether removing the sink was relevant in shifting the energy in there, I'll never know but it certainly did shift. As I mentioned, I'd always been fairly wary of the dark, despite my parents' best efforts but I was about to have genuine reason for this.

The lady that lived in my bedroom started to make herself known not long after the sink was removed. Tucked into the 80's white plywood desk, was a foldable, red wooden chair and this is where she would sit, in the middle of the night. That chair made a certain sound when someone sat on it and in the dead of night, when that sound woke me, I'd know she was there. More often than not, it was just an overwhelming sense of someone sitting there. Only on a few rare occasions did I *'see'* a figure sitting there, head in hands, half slumped over the desk in a long-sleeved, high-necked, full length dress. Having found out later that the house was built on top of an old war hospital's foundations, it may well be that she was a nurse, or perhaps she was just a previous occupant of the house. Either way, she didn't really offer any kind of threat to me, she always just sat there quietly minding her own business but I often sensed she was there.

As a family we often joked about her as we'd all be sitting in the lounge watching TV and often it would sound like someone was walking across my bedroom floor above. She was much more active when there was decorating going on or builders in the house. One of her favourite games, was to switch kettles on and off, particularly if it was builders' tea that was on the menu. Later in life, when I was older and more resilient, we talked about her in more serious tones and it's generally a shared consensus that she lived up there in my bedroom with me, throughout my family's time in that house. I sometimes wonder what became of her and if she's still there, even if she's OK and if the newer occupants know she's there. Living with a spirit in your bedroom certainly inspires a certain amount of interest in the paranormal at the very least, but my interest did also radiate towards divination for all kinds of purposes.

From an early age I had a strong sense of justice,

in fact I believe those very words were uttered by many of my teachers on more than one occasion at parents' evenings. With all that Libran influence in my birth chart, I couldn't bear things to be unfair. This is a pretty big obstacle to try and overcome in a world that is hugely unequal in terms of opportunity, wealth and many other areas. I felt inequality so strongly and deeply within me and still do to this day, always sticking up for the underdog.

I had a pretty *'mainstream'* job for the first half of my life, going to university and becoming a primary school teacher for thirteen years. I still do currently work for the local authority supporting ethnic minorities and particularly Syrian refugees. It was another strange tale that led me to tarot reading and exploring anything spiritual. After thirteen years of teaching I was burnt out and I have huge admiration for anyone in that job. I had no idea what I was going to do if I left teaching but I knew I had to get out.

This was around the period of media reports of chemicals being used in bombing the Syrian people. I remember in the late autumn sitting in front of the news in tears at the images and going to bed praying, that I could help them in some way, particularly the children. I remember thinking that was what I wanted to do - I wanted to help people and particularly children struggling, facing injustices. Cut to the following June when I sat nervously in an interview for a job to support ethnic minorities in schools. Needless to say I got the job and shortly afterwards the team secured a contract as part of a Government resettlement scheme to support Syrian refugee children. Coincidence or fate? I'll let you ponder on that one.

One Christmas, during my teenage years, my dad received a fun tarot deck as a present, something to play around with over the holidays. I was, of course, totally intrigued by it and although it was quite a commercial pack, from a well-known television personality, I loved looking through the cards and at all the imagery. It wasn't long before I purchased my own deck when I was around fourteen years old. It was a Rider Waite Smith deck and came in a snug cardboard box. I bought it from a local stationary shop in Shoreham-By-Sea, where I grew up. Anyone growing up there in the 80's/90's will know which shop I mean!

The pictures, symbolism and numbers all confused me. I tried my best to get to grips with the card meanings using the very small, paper guide book that came with the deck but even many of the key words confused me. The internet was still taking off and I was completely unaware that books surrounding the subject of tarot even existed. It went in a drawer and gathered dust in that bedroom, then it went in a drawer and gathered dust in university halls. Next, it went in a drawer and gathered dust in numerous student houses, then into rented flats and houses, still in a drawer gathering dust. It followed me everywhere I lived and still went in a drawer to gather dust, even in the first house I bought with my now husband. The deck eventually went onto a shelf (an upgrade I guess!) but still gathered dust and followed us once more into our next home which, is our current home. Still it gathered dust, until the day I changed jobs when I was working from 9am until 5pm and had my evenings and weekends back. I finally had time!

I picked up that deck one weekend, the deck that had survived so many life changes and house moves, and began to *'play.'* I also think with a work base in Glastonbury, I'd been reminded of that poor deck and influences from the town had started to rub off on me. It was fascinating, even in the early days, to see how my days would play out compared to the cards I was drawing. As I travelled a lot for work, I also started listening to podcasts on the subject, using the travel time I had in my day to learn new skills. I still read with my original tarot deck from when I was 14 years old. The cards have moved home into a beautiful hand-made wooden box my mum bought me more recently. I do still have the original cardboard box and guide booklet it came in though.

Throughout my teenage years I certainly dabbled with different divination tools. I remember at one time owning a set of runes on pebbles but I have no idea where they ended up. I certainly had an interest in astrology from a very young age. My Nan always bought Old Moore's Almanac and I soon started reading that, later getting my own. I've always been a keen book reader, particularly before bed or first thing in the morning. In fact, even today, I often do tarot readings for myself in bed in the mornings. Usually all these tools and books resided in my bedside cabinet and I've carried this on with all my tarot decks being within easy reach of my bed, much to the dismay of my husband!

Despite exploring a range of different tools I was always leaning back towards my tarot deck, getting it out and just playing around with it. I also had a period in my early teens where I was very much into exploring Ouija boards with friends. This would often involve being huddled around a badly drawn board on an A4 piece of paper, all our index fingers on a glass, asking spirits questions and freaking out as the glass moved in order to answer our queries. I can't remember much of what we asked or what the answers were. I suspect it mostly revolved around boys and for me, probably about whether or not I was ever going to meet and marry Robbie Williams! One memory I do have, having been told yet again that I was not destined to be said Mrs Williams, was who it predicted I was going to marry. (You'll have to forgive my naive focus on *'marriage'* for this story.) I can clearly remember it spelling out a name. We giggled as it spelled the same name as one of our friends. We wondered if their surname was going to follow. It didn't, but gave us a full name of someone we didn't know of. I later met and married the man that held that name.

The Craft was my favourite film through my teenage years. I can't remember how many times I've re-watched it now, even into adulthood. It's still a classic and I won't hear otherwise! I always dreamed of being Nancy, despite (spoiler alert) the less than ideal situation she finally ends up in. I owned a Royal Doulton Bunnykins figurine of a fortune-teller which was a birthday present from my parents and religiously read horoscopes in the papers and magazines. My mood ring was, unsurprisingly, my go-to accessory in the 1990's and I adored my dream catcher. I loved anything celestial, a theme that has carried on into adulthood, with starry earrings, scarfs and more. Whilst some of these things were pretty typical of someone growing up in the 80's and 90's, these are the things I started with. It was these influences that led me to the path I am on now.

The bedroom spirit in my childhood home, wasn't the only spiritual encounter I can remember from my childhood. I shared an interesting experience with my dad one evening whilst driving in the car. My mum and brother were also in the car but didn't seem to have the same experience late that night. We were driving back from a restaurant, as I remember it, my dad was driving and I was looking through the central well of the car, looking through the front window. All of a sudden a family appeared, crossing the road right in front of us, stepping straight out on to the road. There was clearly more than one figure; I can distinctly picture them, even today. My dad had seen them too, as he slammed on the brakes. Yet when we stopped, there was nobody there. I can even remember saying to my dad, *"where did they go?"* Thankfully, there was nobody behind us and we both sat in the car stunned for a moment. It was probably one of the most bizarre visual experiences I have ever had and I'd shared it with someone else. I wasn't crazy, someone else had witnessed this event at exactly the same moment in exactly the same place! My mum and brother had no idea what was going on or why we'd stopped so abruptly. My dad and I couldn't believe that they hadn't seen them! Experiences such as these definitely contributed towards increasing my awareness of all things spiritual and definitely contributed to where I'm at now in my life.

Skip forwards ten years and I was just coming out of Winchester University, as it is now named, after completing a four-year degree in primary school teaching. Yes, it really used to be a four year degree. Somewhere along the way, in-between boys, exams and growing up, my spiritual side had been pushed to the back of my life. It was still there in the background and I loved going to events to see celebrity psychics or having tarot readings but I hadn't picked up that tarot deck in years. There are two readings I had in this period that stick in my mind. They may have been the only two I actually had as, like I say, I was busy on the treadmill of university then straight into my teaching career. One of them was on Brighton seafront: this was just before I headed off to university and I can remember it being just as you'd imagine. A young lady with hooped earrings and a shawl was sitting by a small rounded table along the promenade by the Palace Pier. She was dressed just as you'd imagine a tarot reader would be. I was shopping with my mum and we'd gone for chips on the seafront for lunch on a warm summer's day. This may well have been the first time I actually had a professional reading. It was only brief but I found it fascinating nonetheless and what she predicted totally played out in the coming months. The second reading I had was during my Saturn return at twenty-seven years old. Your Saturn return happens when Saturn is in the same degree in the same sign as where it was when you were born. It happens roughly every twenty-seven to twenty-nine years and brings with it a sense of your own mortality and often includes a period when you make big changes in your life to re-adjust your course, so that your life serves you better.

This reading was with a medium in Southampton, which is where I was teaching and living at the time. As I recall, there weren't any cards used as a tool in this reading at all, it was just the medium and I in a small room above a café. For anyone not familiar, a medium is someone who mediates communication between spirits and the living. I have no memory of why I booked this appointment or of the medium's name but the messages he delivered, backed up by the evidence of things he knew were spot on. This was in the days when I was using a second-hand Blackberry (Google it, I don't mean the fruit variety!), My Space was still around, although I wasn't on it and my Facebook had a profile picture and one status update. He made many predictions during that consultation, some of which he suggested wouldn't play out until the end of my thirties. Sitting here now, typing this at thirty-nine years old, he was totally accurate and very specific. This reading was the catalyst that re-ignited my interest in all things spiritual and particularly divination. The reading was recorded on a cassette but unfortunately, after many house moves, I no longer have it, or anything to play it on. It truly was astounding though.

It wasn't long after that I got my first tattoo. Not many people realise I have it as it's on the upper part of my thigh. Of course, it's of a shooting star, although it's not that detailed, as I was terrified of getting it done and kept it simple. This tattoo was done years before I really learnt the traditional meanings of tarot or started delving properly into astrology. I was already certain, even at this point in my life, that all things mystical would always be a part of my identity. I've never regretted that tattoo, even though it was a bit of an impulse during my Saturn return I was talking about. After I got married I balanced it out a little with a tattoo of an anchor on my ankle. This was a little nod to my heritage but also to my new husband. Whilst most of my astrology chart is filled with planets in the air element, his is much more grounded in earth. I don't have any planets in earth so grounding through meditation, yoga or through getting out in nature is really key for me in staying present. He also helps to keep me balanced.

Back to the theme of Justice. Teaching was something I felt was pre-destined for me. From an extremely young age, even before I went to school, people would ask me what I wanted to be when I grew up. The answer was always the same; I'm going to be a teacher. This never ever changed throughout my whole childhood and into adulthood, so it was easy to make those career decisions in my life. Usually I am quite indecisive with that Libran energy, constantly weighing up different options and going over and over them in my head, yet teaching was always something I was certain of, like an inner knowing. After university I got my first teaching role in Southampton, near the docks. It was hard work but I found it so rewarding teaching pupils from deprived areas. In fighting for the underdog and providing opportunities, those pupils gave me great job satisfaction and made it all worthwhile.

Not long afterwards, I met my husband and relocated to Dorset to be with him. I taught in two schools that were in more affluent areas of Somerset during the following six years. Whilst on a behavioural level this was much easier, unfortunately the job satisfaction and feeling of really making a difference steadily decreased for me. With a change of government and ever increasing demands on teachers and the education system, the joy I felt in my early career, trying to create those equal opportunities for all, was gone. After a spell where my wellbeing really suffered, I resigned from teaching without another job to go to.

My wellbeing had to take priority at this point so I took that leap of faith often talked about in The Fool tarot card. I had no idea where the journey would take me. Whilst I was working out my notice period, a job came up working for an Ethnic Minority Achievement team in education, presenting training days for teachers and supporting pupils. The salary was half my teaching salary but it was a 9am-5pm role, no evenings or weekends, I kept my school holidays and got to use all the skills I'd learnt in my thirteen years of teaching. Plus - perhaps most importantly - it was about striving to provide equal opportunities and support for all. I still continue to work for this amazing team, after getting promoted into an advisory teacher role a year after joining. I was serving my values and my community again and working towards justice for those far less fortunate than myself. Any work I did with Syrian refugee pupils and families was and remains, particularly rewarding. So, I had my wellbeing and my social life back, I had work-life balance for the first time in many, many years. What did I do with all that new time available? I think you can guess...

I can't remember the exact point that I made the decision to unearth those dusty old tarot cards. It certainly wasn't immediately after leaving my teaching position. What may have had an impact was that as part of my new role, I ended up spending a reasonable amount of time in Glastonbury. Glastonbury is certainly a very individual town and not to be confused with Pilton, which is where the famous Performing Arts Glastonbury Festival is held. It has its own vibe going on and a high street filled with independent shops selling all things spiritual such as tarot cards, essential oils, crystals and much more. Many of the cafés are filled with vegan options or are very health conscious and ethical in their service. You're not going to find a chain coffee shop or restaurant on the high street, that's for sure. Of course, I can't fail to mention that all of this lies beneath the Glastonbury Tor with the glorious Chalice Well and gardens alongside it. If you spend any length of time in Glastonbury, I don't think you can fail to have some of that energy rub off on you and it steadily became my favourite place to be. I can only assume that it was this influence that reminded me of my old deck.

I started by pulling a card every morning, trying to intuitively interpret it before turning to the little paper guide book that came with the deck to look at its meaning. That little book left me feeling confused, so it was quickly abandoned. With my new day job came quite a bit of travel. As a team, we were supporting ethnic minority pupils across all schools in Somerset. It was around this time, that I started listening to podcasts about tarot and about the card meanings. Alongside a small selection of books, this was primarily how I started learning about the traditional meanings. By pulling a card each morning, looking up the meanings and reflecting back on how that day went, bit by bit I started to grasp the cards' messages. More often than not, they were surprisingly accurate, spurring me on to learn more. So this was how I started, simply by pulling a card each morning and looking up the meanings.

This wasn't a quick process and went on for a year or two. The more familiar I got with the cards, the more I also started practicing tarot card spreads, starting with the simple three card spread of past, present and future. I didn't complete a *'certification'* in tarot and only actually did one day's formal tarot training to enhance my practice. I've got Mercury retrograde (moving very slowly) in Scorpio in my third house of communication, an indication that I often have to learn things for myself in life. If I had taken a course, I probably wouldn't have taken much of it on board anyway. There is no one way to learn the tarot and no particular certification or qualification to gain, or that you need. What I will say, is that the day's intensive training I did was really valuable in terms of bringing all my knowledge together and confirming my interpretations of the cards. It also gave me valuable insight into the ethical side of professional tarot reading. If you are thinking of using your skills professionally, please, please, please take some time to look into this. There are instances where people may be very vulnerable, not in a good place or may need other professional services rather than a tarot reading. I always have a sheet with local and national links readily to hand to give to anyone who I feel needs a different kind of support. I would suggest you do the same.

Justice drives me just as much in my tarot work as it does in my conventional roles. Using tarot to clarify situations for guidance for all my clients is very rewarding, alongside the belief that at the heart of things, we have certain paths to follow and things to achieve in this lifetime that are meant to be. As a tarot reader, I am certainly not there to tell you what to do and make life decisions for you. However, I can use the tarot as a tool to gain clarity so that you can move forwards more confidently in life with any decision-making. Forewarned is forearmed and looking into the potential future, is part of what I do. I always make clear to clients following a reading, if they sit back, do nothing and solely wait for opportunities to come to them, they are unlikely to build what they desire. They have to put in the work too. The Justice card continues to remind us all in tarot that what you put in, you will eventually be rewarded for, whether it be in this lifetime or the next.

CHAPTER TWO

Present - Four of Wands

The Four of Wands is a card of commitment and celebration with this. It sometimes appears for occasions such as weddings or exchanging on homes but is also a card of recognising achievements that have gone before and that you are working towards in the present. In some senses, it is often a card of things coming together, particularly regarding things you are putting your energy into with those fiery wands. It's certainly a card of more stability on an energetic level. I chose this card to represent the present as I sit here writing, committed to this book and grateful for all my achievements since the early days of teaching to professional tarot reader.

Moving from a conventional role, as a primary school teacher, into spiritual work was a shift that some close to me had to get their head around. I also had to do a lot of inner work in order for me to move forwards in life, living according to my true values and not according to what others expected of me or believed about me. I can now confidently say I don't give a fig what others think about my life choices! I spent too many years, in the lead up to this shift, not living in alignment with my values and beliefs. A good friend once told me that if you don't listen to the universe and your true purpose, then the universe will make you listen. I think that definitely happened to me as I experienced burnout leaving mainstream classroom teaching.

This point in my life was definitely a *'Tower'* moment. In a tarot deck, many people are fearful of this card and the energy it brings. It was definitely a chaotic period in my life, one where things certainly felt like they were crumbling around me and where I felt I lacked any direction. Having been though that experience - and there's been a few other *'Tower'* moments don't get me wrong - I don't find this card as triggering now. I truly believe that whilst it may bring uncomfortable energy, it is very much about the space it creates in your life once the old has been cleared. It's the remaining foundations that you're going to build on that need to be the focus in this card, not the gripping on to what is falling away.

The understanding I gained about myself during this time and the growth that came from it, moved me towards living in alignment with my more authentic self, which in turn, brought me more inner stability, security and commitment that I wouldn't ever lose again. I still need regular time out now to realign and make sure I am following this as it's an on-going process that needs regular maintenance. Now, instead of having to rebuild the whole car, I can just keep on top of re-tuning it!

Moving into this new identity has sometimes been difficult to define. In society, during introductions, we are often asked who we are and what we do. What we *'do'* in society often plays a pivotal role in our identity and how others perceive us. As a tarot reader and astrologer, people do seem to become wary, think you're crazy, or just don't know what to say next. They have an image of me sitting in a darkened room with a shawl over my head, being possessed by spirits as I mix all kinds of animal parts together in a bubbling cauldron. This couldn't be further from the truth.

I live in a normal bungalow, not a cave. I have a husband who is not interested at all in this side of life. I come from a family where my dad was in banking and my mum a secretary, not from a cult and I don't go walking around *'seeing'* dead people - although perhaps there was a flavour of that in my childhood! I also can't tell what you are thinking, so you are perfectly safe speaking to me (and thinking whatever you want). I have no issue if you do resonate with living in a cave or coming from a cult but they are the kind of extreme assumptions about me which simply aren't true. There are, of course, others who are totally on my wavelength, living in conventional ways but interweaving the more spiritual elements of our world within it; these are my people.

Sometimes it is tricky to specifically classify what area I do work in. When you select what area you work in on a social media page, you can choose from a number of options including: astrology, psychic, spirituality, holistic wellbeing or maybe witchcraft. I haven't yet found a label that fully encompasses all of what I do. By ticking *'psychic'* I feel I'm misleading some who think I have a hotline to those who have passed over. By ticking *'holistic wellbeing,'* I feel I am not being clear about the guidance and services I can offer. I took a little time to really delve into some of the definitions of these terms and these are the kinds of things I found:

- **Tarot** – playing cards, used for fortune telling and in certain games.
- **Astrologer** – a person who uses astrology to tell others about their character or to predict their future.
- **Psychic** – someone who claims to use extrasensory perception to identify hidden information.
- **Holistic** – the belief that the parts of something are interconnected rather than the dissection of systems.
- **Wellbeing** – a state of being happy and healthy.
- **Woo Woo** – unconventional beliefs, especially related to spirituality or mysticism, not considered to have any scientific basis.
- **Mysticism** – a vague religious or spiritual belief.
- **Spirituality** – things relating to the human spirit or soul as opposed to physical things.
- **Ethereal** – extremely delicate and light in

a way that seems not to be of this world.
- **Intuitive** – using what you feel to be true without considering conscious reasoning.

There are parts of these definitions that I really resonate with such as spirituality being focused on the human spirit or soul and that the parts of us, in a holistic sense, are interconnected; there are also parts of these definitions that I do not. The fact that tarot is still defined as being part of a game (it does have a history of being used as a game but this was many moons ago), that reasoned consciousness isn't involved or the suggestion that I have some kind of vague religious or spiritual beliefs, is in itself, rather vague. I would argue that even the *'astrologer'* definition doesn't totally feel aligned with services I provide and that I do little *'telling'* and more *'guiding'* of others so that they can find their path themselves. Whilst I can guide, I cannot do any of the work for you. The idea that *'woo woo'* is unconventional irks me too. The rise of interest in our spiritual side is much more widespread than some probably like to admit. Based on these definitions, the category I'd like to be able to select would be:

Spiritually Holistic Tarot Reader and Astrologer...I feel I might be waiting a while to see that specific category.

I couldn't have predicted that I would end up working in spiritual services back when I was teaching. Interestingly though, someone else did - a tarot reader. I went with a friend one Saturday afternoon towards the end of my teaching career, to a local holistic fayre in a local hall. I hadn't had a tarot reading in a long time prior to this and thought what the heck! I certainly needed the guidance at the time. He had no knowledge of me and the reading hadn't been pre-booked. I just sat down when there was a space. He suggested that I would make a huge shift in my career and end up working in a spiritual area. The year following that reading played out exactly as he predicted.

Now that I don't live at home I don't have, as far as I know, any spirits lurking in my bedroom, which isn't to say there haven't been any more recent strange goings-on. Now that I'm married, quite often my husband witnesses some of them too. At the end of July 2019 we had an electrical storm in our small town. I'd certainly never witnessed anything like it before, in fact it was so bright that when it woke me up, it was as if it was daytime with no pauses between the lightning. Whether it was this storm that changed the energy in our house, or whether our home was more open to spiritual energies at this point due to my work, I don't know. After that storm we had a few weeks of some strange stuff going on. It started with my husband's wardrobe doors. At 3am one morning we were both woken by them swinging open. Not just opening a little, but both doors fully opening and waking us up. It had never happened before and has never happened since. We also had an issue with my bedside lamp turning itself on in the night. As it was a touch sensitive one,

I initially thought I was knocking it with my pillow. However, when it started to do it during the daytime too, in front of my very eyes, the lamps had to be replaced with switch ones. We thought we'd been very clever swapping the lamps to switch ones, until that very same night, a dehumidifier in our bedroom turned itself on instead. Somebody up there was having a laugh at our expense! If we have it in our bedroom, from time to time it still does it to this day. I've since smoke cleansed the whole house many times, but it does feel like that storm changed the energy in our home a little.

Not long after, we went to Rome for a city break. As I mentioned, my husband is not really into any kind of spiritual interests, despite the fact he's witnessed some bizarre things with me and here comes another: on our last day, we went to visit some Roman Baths - when in Rome right - we entered an expansive chamber filled with crypts that had been discovered, recovered and preserved for viewing. Echoing in the background, very faintly, we could both hear what sounded like a single monk chanting, then it stopped. There was only one other family in there at the time and they were just leaving. We both heard it, looked everywhere for audio equipment but didn't find any, not even a single speaker. We waited for ages in that room for it to re-start, as an audio track would, but we didn't hear it again.

The last notable experience I had was back in Glastonbury itself, in a car park of all places, as I was leaving an education meeting. I said goodbye to a colleague and started walking towards the boot of my car. I opened it up and then felt a sudden tap on my shoulder and heard someone giggling, really loudly, in my ear. I spun around expecting to see my colleague having a joke but there was no one there. In fact, my colleague was over the other side of the car park putting her bags in her own boot, oblivious to what I was doing. It sent goose bumps over my whole body. All these experiences happened when I was least expecting them and certainly when I wasn't doing any kind of spiritual work. I actually find the spirits pretty calm when I'm working with tarot, possibly because that energy is channelled into the cards.

What all these experiences gave me, was the confirmation of my belief of other spiritual energies in this universe. It made me more committed in following my path and dream of becoming a professional tarot reader and later, astrologer. I was well and truly in that Four of Wands energy, grateful for past achievements and efforts and feeling secure in the knowledge that I was on the right path for me. Other people's opinions of who I was becoming and what I was doing, gradually faded away to nothing as I felt so much more at home with myself and confident in moving forwards.

CHAPTER THREE
Challenges – Two of Pentacles

Becoming a professional tarot reader has not been without its challenges. It hasn't been all spiritual experiences and destiny I'm afraid. At times it's been hard graft getting my name out there and I have definitely had to hustle. There are all kinds of strategies and business approaches promising quick results, how to build huge client bases and earn six-figure sums. Whilst the strategies are often very useful in developing a name, brand and business, there is just no easy way of doing all that. You have to be prepared to get yourself out there and do the hard foundational work towards this. The Two of Pentacles felt like the right card to represent this chapter and these challenges, it's very much a card of balance, particularly in a physical world sense. It can be related directly to building a better work-life balance and navigating some choppy waters in your desire to reach this.

When lockdown hit in the UK in March 2020 I threw all the spare time I'd suddenly gained into building my tarot business. I had no business, sales or marketing experience whatsoever. It was a learning curve even setting up a social media business page - there was so much to learn. I lived and breathed my business throughout the lockdown periods, I went to marketing webinars, watched videos on how to take great social media photographs and enrolled myself in a holistic business academy for a short period. Whilst I absolutely wanted to serve others using tarot, I wasn't going to be able to do this if nobody knew who I was or how to get in contact with me. The business side of what I do is equal in importance to the services I provide, so that I can help as many people as possible and make these services as accessible as they can be - this was particularly important to me.

As you've already discovered, I come from a very conventional background and feel that we can all have tarot readings and use astrology to enhance our everyday lives, without it being considered part of some kind of underground sub-culture. I've always tried to make myself as approachable as possible and have worked hard to express this through any advertising or social media presence. I hope this is the impression I give, as it's a message that is true. Alongside this, I've also worked hard to provide accessible and useful content for my followers such as the weekly guidance videos. So behind all of the spiritual work, there was a lot of learning and business work going on as well. Anyway, enough about the business side.

I live in the smallest town in Dorset, right on the border with Somerset. Whilst I grew up in a very liberated area of England with a variety of cultures and sub-cultures, where I live now is much quieter. Reading tarot and astrology charts is much more commonplace in Brighton, or is it just spoken about more? It was certainly quite a nerve-racking experience the first time I hit publish in the local community group advertising my services. I'm certain there were some who thought I'd finally lost the plot and that it would all be some kind of *'phase'* that I was going through.

Challenging those initial pre-conceptions of what a tarot reader does and what type of person they are, was a mindset obstacle I faced. Lots of my initial social media posts included statements about what I could do - help provide clarity for making decisions for the future - as well as statements about what I couldn't do - tell you the winning lottery numbers, if only I could! For me, I had already done the inner work involved in *'coming out'* as a tarot reader, astrologer and all round spiritual person. Through perseverance I found my people and I found my customers. The more I put myself out there, the more people opened up to me saying how interested they were and how they'd be fascinated to either have their cards read or birth chart interpreted. Bookings steadily increased, firstly online during the first lockdown, then later in-person, during periods when lockdown was eased.

I had unknowingly timed the opening of my business in a period where people were really looking for direction and guidance on a more spiritual level. The pandemic and various lockdowns left many with lots of time on their hands for the first time in a long while. People had time to reflect and take stock of their lives. Many were having to make enforced changes to careers and work, some were finding that post lockdowns, they actually didn't want their old jobs or way of life back.

Some relationships also didn't stand the test of time during this period. More and more bookings focused on where clients should direct their energy next and what their new future held for them. It was a fabulous start to my business and the experience I was gaining from reading the variety of situations in this period was so valuable and rewarding. It was a privilege to be able to help others during such a tricky time.

Providing readings online, only proved to be a challenge for the first few weeks of lockdown, whilst everyone got Zoom and other online platforms setup. Once these were established and being widely used, most people were more than happy for services to be online, many asking me if tarot could really be done online without them present or drawing their own cards. In my experience, it has not made any difference in the accuracy of my readings, either through Zoom or when voice-recording a reading to be emailed out to clients. Again, this was more about mindset and getting the message out there that tarot could go ahead online.

I always ensure the cards are cleansed before each reading, either through smoke cleansing or through sound vibrations and will always concentrate on the client's energy when shuffling. I will also focus this energy when drawing cards for them. I don't think online services will ever fully take the place of a face-to-face reading and the experience the client gets but in this situation, where there wasn't a choice, it came as close as possible.

Work-life balance and keeping my energy aligned has been an interesting journey and probably one I'm still on. Picking up on all the energy from others can sometimes leave me feeling quite drained. Halloween fell on a Saturday in 2020 and we weren't in too tight a lockdown at that point in the year. I had a fully booked afternoon of tarot readings that day, one after the other and was absolutely wiped out by it. I have learnt that I need regular breaks and time between clients to reset myself and have a good cleanse. Having a salt bath after a long afternoon seeing clients really helps to ground me. I find meditation great before starting readings, to channel energy, but find it trickier to focus a frazzled mind into meditation afterwards. I'm also usually ravenous after a few appointments so need some good, hopefully healthy, snacks ready for me, although anyone who knows me well knows I'm always hungry regardless of what I've been doing.

I still try and fit in too many readings into too little time sometimes, even today, not giving myself enough headspace between them. I have quite an *'I can'* attitude to bookings so it's a continuous challenge to ensure I'm staying grounded. In my birth chart I don't have any planets in earth signs and many in air signs. Meditating and doing lots of yoga helps to balance this but I think it will be something I'll always have to manage and keep an eye on. I'm in my head a lot! The balance being sought in that Two of Pentacles will probably always be a feature in my life.

Moving out of lockdown for a period allowed me to get back to some in-person readings and consultations. At exactly the time I was putting myself out there as a tarot reader, a friend of mine was also looking to expand her business. In my immediate local area, we were lacking a little in holistic businesses and she was setting up a centre where many therapists with a range of skills could work. I jumped at the chance to get some regular slots booked up. I soon found myself fully booked proving there was certainly a demand for these kinds of services. The more bookings I had, the more people told their friends too, who in turn booked in. Whilst having a great social media following is brilliant in terms of how many people you can reach and help, there is nothing more powerful than a testimonial from someone who has seen you in person.

Building a local reputation like this was invaluable during this period. Some came due to a high interest in spirituality, some came who were just curious as to how it all worked. I welcome all and enjoy exploring with those curious just as much as with enthusiasts. As more and more people realised we were open and available at the time for in-person slots, the busier I became. In came that Two of Pentacles energy again. The more I used tarot to serve others, the less I was doing my own inner work and self-care. I quickly learnt that I did sometimes need to say no to late night appointments, or when I really didn't have the space. I'm always more than happy to recommend others who might be able to fit them in sooner when this is the case. It was a great problem to have though and I will always be grateful for the opportunity given to me by my friend and getting my first step on the ladder in her therapy centre.

CHAPTER FOUR

Mind – Ace of Swords

On a mind level I chose the Ace of Swords. The swords suit in tarot often represents what's happening on a mind level, when reading a spread. There can be some trickier themes when we see swords cards, particularly if we pull the Three of Swords representing disappointment and perhaps heartbreak. However, working through those areas often leads to greater understanding of ourselves and also towards making leaps forwards, in terms of clarity, understanding and self-acceptance. This is why I have chosen one of the more positive swords cards to represent my journey of the mind.

Working with tarot and astrology has meant that I have had to do lots of self-reflection; in fact, essentially this is what we are doing when working through a tarot spread or when looking at a natal chart. We delve into the strengths and weaknesses using these tools, looking at how best to explore talents but also how to manage weaker areas so we can work with them positively, which has meant I have become clearer about who I am and what I stand for. This hasn't been easy work, especially when I made that big career shift away from whole class teaching. It is hard and tiring work. Anyone who suffers with anxiety or depression will tell you that the mental exhaustion that sometimes accompanies this can be crippling. However, this kind of work very much comes with the territory when learning how to use a divination tool such as tarot. It is almost impossible to learn without delving into your own shadow side and we all have one. Often when I see clients, unless they have made an appointment due to curiosity, it's because there is a pressing issue in their life or they are doing this kind of shadow work and reflecting on the direction they are taking. What I will say, is that it has given me insight into how similar we humans really are, often struggling with similar themes or wanting to know similar things about ourselves. Meeting such a variety of people is definitely a perk of tarot reading. It has helped me to put my own issues into perspective, see things from different perspectives and realise that we are all human and not alone.

The Ace of swords is also associated with new beginnings, as are all the aces. Applying the swords suit to this, a new beginning of the mind is often on the horizon, should you pull this card. This could be related to your mindset and how you are thinking about things, or might be related to learning in some way. In order to read tarot and then astrology professionally, I certainly had to do lots of learning.

Everyone learns in their own way, some through audio, some through reading, some need more practical ways to learn. If you are entering into tarot training, pick what is right for you and what will work best. No one method will be better, or more recognised, than any other. As I mentioned, the majority of my early learning came from podcasts on longer car journeys. I can't recommend enough gaining a great knowledge based foundation in tarot when learning to interpret the cards. I read about the numerology involved, the symbols and the links to Kabbalah. I listened to podcasts surrounding the suits, how the cards linked to astrology, the structure of the Major Arcana cards and many more topics surrounding tarot. By getting that foundational knowledge in place first, almost obsessively, I could then apply it when reading intuitively.

What do I mean by reading the cards intuitively? Armed with all that knowledge, I no longer needed the guidebooks anymore and could pull cards knowing the traditional meanings but what did I perceive the cards to be telling me about my specific question or situation? This is where the combination of intuition and knowledge make for clearer messages. Sometimes I am drawn to the numbers in a spread, sometimes to the symbolism or the suits. Not every single aspect of each card is necessarily important in every interpretation. I read using a combination of these factors, using the knowledge to back up what I am sensing and intuitively feeling from a card, or combination of cards; this was how I developed my skills as a tarot reader, over the course of a few years. There were occasions when I fell out with the cards, usually due to me misinterpreting the messages and then getting frustrated that things didn't play out as expected. Sometimes when this happened I wouldn't touch the cards for a couple of weeks but I always went back to them again.

I love learning and don't think I will ever stop learning new skills or information related to tarot and astrology. If you enter into the spiritual realm professionally there will always be new things to learn and having a growth mindset is essential, one where you are open to learning new things all the time. There will be times when a card will show up in a completely different expression of itself, yet make perfect sense in the context and to a particular client. I've had questioners who have drawn all the cards featuring angels in a spread and then they have explained a story where a medium had not long previously said that their mother was around them and they just had to look for all the angels. I've also had readings where cards have come up that can't be placed at the time of the reading but their energy soon came in. Once I was doing a quick read for a colleague at lunch and they pulled The Tower card. She couldn't place the card when it was drawn and just as I was explaining this energy can sometimes appear like a bolt from the blue, she received a telephone call. Her niece had suddenly gone into labour early and as it played out, became quite unwell. Thankfully, she did make a full recovery and baby was just fine.

Another time, I pulled The Devil card for a client

in a future position and was discussing the shadow side of ourselves attached to this card, from perhaps over-thinking to extremes such as addiction. She couldn't place what this might be related to and left the reading pondering what was to come. As the next month or two played out, she was involved in a car accident and became reliant on painkiller medication. She, too, has recovered well you'll be pleased to hear.

On a positive note, I've seen The Empress come up in a spread, accompanied by The Sun and predicted upcoming pregnancies. I've seen The Chariot appear when someone doubted a house move, suggesting they definitely needed to go for it. They did and the move was successful. However, I've also seen it appear when someone was making the shift into a job where they could work from home. To me, it is always fascinating to see how the cards choose to express themselves and surrounding cards will always give plenty of clues.

I don't like to know too much about clients before I see them for tarot readings. I am never going to spend my time looking for the background of people on social media in order to *'cheat'* in some way. I would rather the cards spoke for themselves and I let them do the talking in disproving any doubts clients may have. It also makes the reading much more enjoyable for me, like uncovering a mystery and I get to play detective for an hour or so with tools of divination.

CHAPTER FIVE

Heart – Ace of Cups

Tarot and astrology has brought me so many new beginnings on so many levels, that I've chosen another ace card to represent my heart. I'm hogging all the aces in this book. Having come to terms with leaving mainstream teaching after so many years, I think it's fair to say my heart was slightly (!) broken and I had no idea where I was heading.

Learning tarot, just for myself in the early days, helped give me tools to use for reflection and healing when I was in the middle of what felt like personal chaos. Tarot allowed me to look at things from different perspectives. It brought new prompts for me to explore and contemplate and really helped me through this period. Through hard work and sheer determination, I did get my new beginning on a heart level and got through that time in my life.

Often the Ace of Cups is linked to romance or a new love interest, but it is also about the relationship we have with ourselves. I needed to speak to myself more kindly and the tarot supported me in understanding myself with more clarity. I became more accepting of myself as I am and more patient. I also felt that I was finally just being me, weird quirks and all. The more spiritual practices I learnt about, the more I felt like I was coming home and finally finding a place that was for me. I am now fiercely protective of the peace I've found through tarot and of course, astrology. I won't let others disturb that peace and whilst I'm more than happy for them to give alternative views on my more spiritual side, I know the value it brings to my life, I am secure in that.

Tarot also made a little girl's dream come true. As a child, whilst I loved all things spiritual, I saw them as something you do as a hobby or indulge in whilst in the privacy of your home. Being a professional tarot reader wasn't something I perceived as a career path in the 1980's or 90's. It seemed a whimsical fantasy and something that was only in movies or books. I would watch those movies and read those books and dream of being the tarot reader or witchy character. I envied how they were portrayed, listening to and trusting their intuition whilst using all kinds of divination tools. My favourite part of the film *'Robin Hood – Prince Of Thieves'* was when they showed the Sheriff of Nottingham's mother as an old crone, breaking an egg and bone casting into it to foretell what was to play out. That scene was only around a minute long but I can still see it clearly in my mind's eye now. I wanted to be that witch up in the tower in that castle. Teaching was a big part of my life story and not something I will ever regret doing but I felt I'd achieved all that I'd wanted out of the career in thirteen years and was ready to fulfil another dream. In being determined in those early days to learn each individual tarot card meaning and being patient with myself in that process, I worked hard to make that girl's dream come true. I also wanted to be Kylie Minogue but I think that position remains taken!

The point when I really felt I had succeeded in manifesting that dream was when I began reading in-person at the therapy centre. To have business cards, leaflets, be advertised on the website as well as having my own website, really brought home how far I had come from the early days of playing with the cards late at night with friends over a bottle of wine. It hit me the first night after I had finished all my clients and I took a moment to appreciate that achievement. When you're starting a business of any kind, so much work goes on in the background. I was so grateful to be in such a better place than I had been three years previously and I had to almost pinch myself as I had made that whimsical fantasy a reality for myself. I don't ever take for granted the clients I serve and whilst it's so rewarding to be able to help them, every appointment I have also supports building my dream job. It's an absolute privilege to be in that position.

Lots of the skills that I learnt as a teacher were very transferable into my new role. I often think if you've been a teacher, the life experience you gain alone is invaluable, not to mention the flexibility, people skills, public speaking, academic writing and the organisational, financial, multi-tasking and problem-solving skills you develop. I could go on with that list of skills but I think you get my point. All those years of tactful parents' evenings meant that I could deliver trickier messages that the cards were showing in a diplomatic manner. It also meant I didn't shy away from those conversations either. Passing on messages from cards such as The Sun or The Star is always a pleasure but the real tact and skill comes when you have to convey the not-so-great stuff to an already concerned client.

Clients will always get the whole truth the cards are showing me in a reading. They, of course, always have free will to change their path having received that guidance. Even if things do play out as predicted, we always have a choice in how we react to events or situations in life. Tarot will only show the potential of what is to come should you continue down a certain path when it comes to the choices we make. Teaching also enabled me to read tarot with positivity and with compassion. Having been through some rather trying times in my life and feeling like I'd hit rock bottom, I have nothing but empathy and compassion for clients who are struggling. Only life experience and the opportunity to meet so many people through teaching gave me those skills. It allows me to connect to clients not just through the cards but on a basic human and heart level too.

CHAPTER SIX

Body – Eight of Pentacles

I chose the Eight of Pentacles to represent this chapter of my story as it is the card of apprenticeship. It is about learning your craft, developing it and eventually mastering it. As I've already mentioned, lots of self-study and practice went into becoming a tarot reader. It really did feel like an apprenticeship of sorts, one that I was working on alone but was very focused on nonetheless. Now you'd think that all you'd need to become a tarot reader would be a deck and off you go but there were lots of other tools I found I needed, as well as knowledge of practices such as smoke cleansing. Social media played a huge part in setting up my business, as did personal skills such as having to be patient and not expect immediate results whilst I figured out what worked and what didn't work for both me and my clients.

I still predominantly read tarot with the Rider Waite Smith deck I bought as a teenager. It is my most go-to deck and the one I feel most connected with, partly because it has been with me for so long. However, I really feel that tarot readers do need at least a couple of decks for a few reasons. Firstly, I like to give my clients a choice of deck when they come to me and I let them choose which they are drawn to. It also gives clients more ownership in how the reading is conducted, allowing them to select a deck they feel is going to speak to them most clearly. Many do choose the traditional Rider Waite Smith deck but some do feel the images, illustrated in 1909, do not represent them, particularly when it comes to ethnicity, gender and relationships. I always have a more diverse deck available so that all clients can feel represented and comfortable coming to me for readings. I also like to have a more non-gender specific deck to choose from too, perhaps one based on animals, or a pips deck that is based on the numeric system displaying the numbers on Minor Arcana cards rather than people.

Another reason I recommend having a few decks available during a reading is so that you can also change decks should you wish. Sometimes I get the feeling that I'm not getting much clarity from a deck, or messages are becoming confusing. This might be because it needs a good cleanse, or because it has already been used a lot on a particular day and is worn out. I'm certain that the decks have their own characters! Having at least one other deck on hand means I can quickly switch to another which often brings a fresh energy to a reading. The trouble with buying tarot decks is that it quickly becomes quite addictive as there are so many beautiful decks out there. I often go through phases with my decks when certain decks will call to me for particular clients or during specific periods. Alongside tarot decks, it can sometimes be beneficial to have an oracle deck to hand too. Oracle decks don't stick to the same systems as tarot, but this can mean they bring a new perspective on reading. It can be quite nice to finish a reading with an overall oracle card, such as an affirmation or colour card, as a final note. It can really round off the reading and indicate the session has finished. I don't subscribe to the myths that you have to be bought your decks or that they need storing in a particular manner. I choose decks that I am drawn to and keep them in a way that feels right to me. My Rider Waite Smith deck is in a wooden box but I have a deck in a black velvet pouch, one in a cotton pouch and one in a knitted tarot bag I made myself. Some remain in their original boxes and I use all of them effectively.

As well as owning the decks, I also needed to ensure I had an adequate way of cleansing my decks and tools, helping create the right atmosphere for a reading. A common way to cleanse decks is through smoke cleansing. This is where herbs, often sage, are burned and the cards are passed through the smoke to cleanse them. The same process can be carried out with incense or by using a smoke cleansing stick. Other methods of cleansing I use are sound vibrations using chime bells, bathing decks under full moon light and when I am short on time, giving a deck three firm taps on the back. All of these will reset the energy of the deck, clearing any energy left behind from myself or previous clients.

I researched and learnt about all of these methods and more when I was learning tarot in order to get the best out of any readings I was undertaking. I also cleanse myself between each reading, if possible, so that I don't pick up and take on clients' energy from readings. Alongside this, I also make sure I am protecting my energies during a reading and am often seen wearing my large unakite pendant.

Whilst you can perform a tarot reading anywhere from your lawn to your dining room table, I find that by having some trusty tools around me, my readings are much clearer. I like to have a good quality tarot cloth to lay the tarot cards out on. I think that if you respect your tarot cards and treat them well, you will receive that respect back and readings will be clearer. I have a black velvet cloth with an astrology pattern on it that I frequently use to lay cards out on. As I'm from a seaside town I also like to have some of my roots and personality involved in the presentation of any card photographs so I usually have a selection of shells nearby that often make it into customer pictures. It's like a little calling card of mine.

It became quite clear early on in my journey that social media was going to play a big role in becoming a tarot reader. This has been further emphasised by the lockdowns and expansion of tools such as Zoom. Launching a business of any kind at the moment without social media would be extremely tricky so I had to quickly start mastering the best ways to market myself on different platforms. When I started my journey, I only had a Facebook page and worked solely on this. I didn't even have a mailing list at this point and relied solely on people stumbling across my page and giving me a *'like'* or a follow. Needless to say, this strategy was not particularly successful and I quickly realised my social media presence was going to be integral to any transformation and in getting my services out there. I slowly started joining local Facebook groups and Spiritual groups and posting more on these to spread the word about my services. The more I shared, the more followers I gained so I had, at least in the short term, found something that was working to get my name known. In the early days of my page, I posted pretty inconsistently and lacked any real technological know-how in producing good quality posts that would engage followers. I also had to find the balance between staying true to my values with the content I was delivering whilst also making sure that my marketing was being noticed so that people could access my services if desired.

Various social media studies have suggested that it takes someone around seven views of a post before they actually really take note of it. Based on this, I knew I had to turn it up a notch and turn it up I did - perhaps turning that dial a little too high at times. Sorry to anyone on my mailing list that got bombarded in the early days! I like to think I've found the right blend now; a mixture of valuable content for followers plus a few advertisements in there every now and then. It certainly took some playing with though.

Learning, just like the apprenticeship in that Eight of Pentacles, was a big part of developing my social media presence. If only I could have just let the tarot cards do all the talking with clients just *'finding'* me hey? During the lockdowns it did seem that Facebook was largely being used by an older generation, in which I include myself. Many seemed to be shifting over to Instagram and a much younger audience was on TikTok. The first time I set up Instagram I actually deleted the account after a few days, thinking it was social media overload being on two platforms. However, it wasn't long before I made a second attempt and this time I kept the page, which is still live today. This was another learning curve with a whole different platform that worked in a very different way. The investment of time did pay off though and I quickly grew in line with my Facebook page. TikTok came next and my account is, at the point of writing this, only a week old. So here I am again, reading blogs and joining free webinars all about another platform. Again, there were different tricks to this platform that I needed to master and get to grips with. So far, I've had a mix of successes and failures but I've definitely learnt a lot in seven days. Watch this space!

I will always be learning in the spiritual profession. Whether it's a new social media platform, a new tarot deck to get to grips with, or a new aspect on an astrology chart, it is a never-ending path. There probably won't ever be that one moment of mastery that might follow the hard work of the Eight of

Pentacles but there will be huge accomplishments along the way. It's a profession and a skill where you have to enjoy the journey and the insights these bring, rather than getting to a final point and considering yourself a master.

CHAPTER SEVEN

Soul – The High Priestess

There really was only one card that I could choose from a tarot deck to represent my soul. The High Priestess is a very spiritual card. Whilst The Hierophant speaks of more structured teaching, learning and religion, The High Priestess is highly connected to the Moon, often depicted with it in tarot decks. She is traditionally a very feminine character, moving with the ebb and flow of that lunar energy. She lets her intuition guide the way in making decisions or supporting others. She trusts her instincts and inner wisdom and is able to channel out any outside distractions, seeing the bigger picture. She often sits between two pillars, one black and one white, representing that she knows life is not black and white and that somewhere in-between lies that spiritual knowing. Trusting your instincts can sometimes be tricky but The High Priestess can distinguish between what is an inner truth and what is simply the *'what if'* fear that we all go through at times.

I think we all have a High Priestess within us, but it's our individual choice as to whether we allow her to guide us or not. When I was teaching full-time I don't think I had enough headspace to hear her voice. As I moved into a more spiritual role in my life, hearing her voice and trusting my inner wisdom became an absolute pleasure. I can still sometimes get wrapped up in everyday stresses and chores but do now ensure I make time to listen to my inner High Priestess on a regular basis.

My husband and I own a 1970's Sierra Yellow, (although it looks orange), Bay Window VW Campervan. Now you might be thinking that this does not belong in a chapter all about the soul but hear me out. When I was a full-time teacher we had dreams of owning a campervan. My husband had got through many rusty beetles that were unbearably loud, bumpy, low and that inevitably he would eventually get bored of and sell on. They were acting as a compromise as they kept him happy but didn't involve the commitment, time and love that a campervan was truly going to need. I also spent far too many of my weekends as a teacher exhausted or doing work and couldn't see how we would get any use out of a campervan. Holidays for me needed to be cosy, all-inclusive hotels where I could truly rest and not lift a finger.

The everyday demands of our lifestyle put that dream to the back of our minds over and over again, even after a health scare. When I left teaching I had the space to get back in touch with what was truly going to make my soul sing, and it turned out part of that was a campervan. We initially owned a white

1980's VW T25 for any VW enthusiasts out there and we were pretty pleased with that at the time but it was so slow! We would have to plan in a lot of extra time for journeys and were very relieved that we made it from Dorset to Wales and back again one August. As time went on, we saved up some money and got an upgrade.

When I was teaching, we had savings but just didn't have the energy to spend or enjoy them. Life revolved around the long working week I was doing and anything like housework or errands was crammed into the weekends. I lost sight of what truly made me happy and our campervan has been a huge part of getting back in touch with that and my soul. It also gave me more time by the sea. When I started tarot reading professionally I named the business *'Tarot Tidings UK'* with a play on the word tide and tidings, linking both my seaside heritage and the messages tarot brings. As things developed and I also became an astrologer I dropped this business name but the beach will always be important to me. I grew up living right by it, spent summers on it and just by being near it, my soul is soothed. Having the water sign Pisces for my moon is probably also a part of this, with our moon being related to our emotions and our emotional and physical needs. The campervan is a huge part of my life and I can't imagine us not having one now. The joy and the feeling of being able to just get away but in our own little moving home, can't be beaten. Although don't get me wrong, when we've been away for a couple of weeks, it's nice to come home too, to a larger bed and home comforts. It definitely makes festivals more luxurious though.

One thing that tarot allowed me to do on a soul level, initially when I left teaching and still today, is to be able to channel out any outside distractions. It allows me to focus purely on my intuition, inner knowing and what makes my soul happy. When I am in our spare room with candles lit, incense burning and have just done a meditation, I am able to concentrate just on what the cards are telling me and work with their guidance. Whilst having that gave me a pleasant distraction from outside influences when things felt like they were all crumbling down around me, it also gave me the freedom to delve within and a tool to do this with. Tarot and astrology are forms of divination. They are part of the practice of seeking knowledge of the future or the unknown by supernatural means. Sometimes, the unknown just needs to be tapped into and I have found that tarot is the tool that best works for me to do this. Tarot may not give me all the full answers but it does give me extra guidance and insight to explore my inner world and the unknown.

Despite doing lots of work on being myself and following my true path, I still suffer from imposter syndrome at times, just like everybody else. When I first started reading professionally, I worried that I wouldn't be a good enough reader and that everyone would be wanting their money back. I worried that I didn't belong in the spiritual community coming from a very conventional background and coming to tarot reading relatively later in life, at the grand old age of 35. I worried that I'd made a mistake starting to read professionally and who was I to think that I could just do that? It was all imposter syndrome and The High Priestess is always a card that reminds us to remain in touch with instincts and to trust them. It felt right and I didn't know where the journey was going to lead, I didn't know I would be sitting here in my kitchen whilst hubby makes lasagne, writing a book. I did however, know that it felt right when things had felt wrong for too long for me.

CHAPTER EIGHT

Potential Future – The World

Whenever I'm reading tarot I will always say *'potential'* future instead of implying that it is totally set in stone. The future position in a tarot spread, for me, represents what will happen should you continue on the path you are currently on. I do still think you have a certain degree of free will. If you choose to stay in bed, take no action and wait for a good card to come into your life, you're unlikely to see that play out, so I don't use the term as a get out clause for my readings in any way, it's more because at the end of the day, you have the final say on what you choose to do. Many readers may disagree and suggest destiny is at large and you cannot avoid that. When doing astrology consultations, I would take that line but tarot feels to me to be much more about guidance and a tool to help us access our inner realm and potential.

When choosing a card for this chapter, I aimed high; I've never lacked ambition in my life! The World is a card of achievement, joy and infinite possibilities. It's the only card where a figure is traditionally dancing, representing that happiness and for the future, lots more happiness would be lovely. I do want to achieve things with my business though. I can't ever see myself not doing tarot and astrology now, even if it takes a backseat through different periods in my life, before re-emerging. I want to write a book, good job really as we're nearly at the end of part one of this one now. I want to read tarot or astrology for some celebs. I'd love to have my own tarot deck produced, although I am no artist. I want to keep helping people. If you're reading this now, it looks like I at least achieved writing the book, which is worthy of The World card in itself, I think. Fingers crossed I am continuing to help people too. The World can also be a card of travel. Sitting here typing this during the third UK lockdown, travel sounds like absolute heaven at the moment. Who knows, I can definitely do this job from anywhere in the world over online platforms, so maybe I will get to travel whilst I work in the future.

Something that is very recent to me, at the time of writing, is Clubhouse. By the time you're reading this, perhaps it has all been a social media flash in a pan but at the moment it seems to be ever growing. I'm sure, even by the time this book is published, it will have all evolved again and there'll be a new trend or platform on offer. Whilst I'd love not to be on there, I doubt many of you reading this would be doing so if I wasn't keeping on top of my social media. So here's to whatever comes next on a technological front, maybe I'll be doing tarot online in 3D for clients, with them wearing 3D glasses. If you're reading this and it's a thing, you heard it here first!

I'm very much a one-woman show in my business as working in the spiritual realm is very personal. Often clients are coming to me with their deepest fears, worries or situations that are going on in their private lives. I don't take the decision they've made to confide in me lightly. As I've already mentioned, everything discussed is completely confidential and trust is integral to all my readings and consultations. It's also always a privilege to be chosen to read for someone as this is quite a personal decision by a client. They need to feel that they are going to be comfortable speaking about their life with me, a complete stranger. This is a very personal choice and I have had to do a lot of work to make sure I don't take it personally if people choose to go elsewhere for readings. In the future I can't see this changing. If anything, post lockdowns, it feels like the human need to communicate on a personal level with others is growing stronger. I will always be providing a very personal service that will focus on clients' personal needs.

That's not to say there won't be other branches growing in the future though. This book, for example, is one of a couple of physical products I have produced. My online beginner's astrology course was the first thing I produced that has video modules to follow but didn't need me to be ever present, in order to provide transformation for my clients. There is a limit to how many hours there are in a day. Offering some services that don't need me to be there in person all the time brings me a happier work-life balance. Moving forward, I'm sure there'll be a few more things like this coming out.

Finally, I guess I want to be that naked figure on The World card, dancing in sheer joy. However the world around me changes and whatever the future brings, I hope I am that character...but maybe with some clothes on!

Striding out on my own.

Beach days in France in the 80's.

Goofing around in Florida as a teenager.

Getting my surf on in Croyde, Devon.

A muddy Glastonbury Festival.

Vintage Glam at Nostalgia Festival.

When in Cuba...Club Tropicana, Havana.

Paddle boarding off Portland.

The Roman Baths, Rome.

The house with my 'lady.'

Part 2

Part two of this book is focused primarily on all the basics you need to begin tarot reading for yourself. In the next section, you will find key words for all the cards, numerology, astrological links and many other tips so you can get tarot reading quickly and efficiently. All too often people think that they need a really deep understanding of all the cards before they can even begin using them. However, the best way to learn tarot is to just do it! Use the information in the rest of this book as a simple beginner's guide and then get practicing.

There will be many cards that you will develop your own meanings for and don't forget to trust your intuition and what you are seeing. There are times when I pull a card and am drawn to a particular part of the image, or a colour. Go with these signs and see what you are drawn to when you've selected a card. There are no rules, there are no official qualifications. Whilst it's great to attend courses for your own development, they are not compulsory. Play to your strengths when learning tarot. In order to build confidence though, it will be practice, practice, practice. Make sure you get some feedback too, you want to know how the reading played out in real life, whether you were accurate or not. It's all useful information.

CHAPTER NINE

Major Arcana

0 **The Fool** – Big new journey, trust the process, leap of faith.
1 **The Magician** – Manifesting, dreams to reality, vision, goals.
2 **The High Priestess** – Intuition, subconscious, meditation, divine feminine.
3 **The Empress** – Abundance, creativity, fertility, growth.
4 **The Emperor** – Ambition, boundaries, determination, leadership.
5 **The Hierophant** – Teacher, healer, counsellor, inner wisdom.
6 **The Lovers** – Harmonious relationships, choices, love, inner truth.
7 **The Chariot** – Success, victory, movement, balance, travel.
8 **Strength** – Willpower, inner strength, grace, courage.
9 **The Hermit** – Solitude, retreat, inner light, unconscious mind.
10 **Wheel of Fortune** – Prosperous change, resilience, appreciation.
11 **Justice** – Equality, law, karma, balance, restoration.

12 **The Hanged Man** – Peace, self-care, being present, meditation, welcome delays.

13 **Death** – Change, transformation, endings, beginnings, letting go.

14 **Temperance** – Alchemy, patience, blending, process, transformation.

15 **The Devil** – Shadow side, materialism, unhealthy habits, power struggles.

16 **The Tower** – Bolt from the blue, clearing out, chaos, dramatic change.

17 **The Star** – Wishes, freedom, inspiration, time to shine, rejuvenation.

18 **The Moon** – Imagination, unclear direction, restlessness, intuition, cycles.

19 **The Sun** – Joy, happiness, fun, new perspectives, optimism.

20 **Judgment** – Higher purpose, true path, reflection, rebirth, choice.

21 **The World** – Accomplishment, achievement enlightenment, success, travel.

CHAPTER TEN

Minor Arcana

Wands (Fire)
– Energy, Passion, Projects, Action

- **Ace of Wands** – New beginning related to energy, passion, project.
- **Two of Wands** – Planning, broadening horizons, pushing yourself.
- **Three of Wands** – Journey, exploration, firm foundation, travel.
- **Four of Wands** – Commitment, celebration, stability, structure.
- **Five of Wands** – Competition, pettiness, competitiveness, squabbles.
- **Six of Wands** – Recognition, reward, success, glory.
- **Seven of Wands** – Upper hand, self-worth, fighting for yourself.
- **Eight of Wands** – Quick action, progress, things coming together.
- **Nine of Wands** – Guarded, paranoia, wounded warrior, walls.
- **Ten of Wands** – Heavy burden, overwhelm, stress, responsibilities.

- **Page of Wands** – Message about a passion or project, opportunity.
- **Knight of Wands** – Adventure, travel, fun, action, bold, courage.
- **Queen of Wands** – Positivity, enthusiasm, power, passion, cosmology, boundaries.
- **King of Wands** – Confident leader, taking the lead, inspiring leader, successful.

Cups (Water)
– Heart, Emotions, Feelings, Creativity

- **Ace of Cups** – New beginning of abundance, love, self-care.
- **Two of Cups** – Healing, reunion, equality, love.
- **Three of Cups** – Shared celebration, fertility, companionship.
- **Four of Cups** – Missing an offering, disgruntled, broaden perspectives.
- **Five of Cups** – Grief, building with what remains, release losses.
- **Six of Cups** – Nostalgia, inner child, reflection, ancestors.
- **Seven of Cups** – Possibilities, illusion, weighing up pros and cons.
- **Eight of Cups** – New journeys, moving on, strength, assessing what serves you.
- **Nine of Cups** – Wishes, manifesting, fruition of dreams.
- **Ten of Cups** – Contentment, happiness, gratitude, happy home life.

- **Page of Cups** – Message of love, pleasant news, surprising news, creative opportunity.
- **Knight of Cups** – Act of love, support, care, going the extra mile.
- **Queen of Cups** – Compassionate, sensitive, caring, motherly, nurturing a creative project.
- **King of Cups** – Balanced emotions, leader of emotional support, sensitive leader.

Swords (Air)
– Mind, Thought, Intellect, Learning

- **Ace of Swords** – New beginnings related to mind, intellect.
- **Two of Swords** – Guarding, choosing not to see, ambivalence.
- **Three of Swords** – Disappointment, heartbreak, let down, sadness.
- **Four of Swords** – Time out, rest, self-care, healing, recharge.
- **Five of Swords** – Anger, haste, spite, unforeseen consequences.
- **Six of Swords** – Difficult decision, moving to peace, moving on, accepting help.
- **Seven of Swords** – Strategy, tact, sneakiness, deceit.
- **Eight of Swords** – Trapped feelings, fearful, a need to take back your power.
- **Nine of Swords** – Anxiety, what if's, sleeplessness, despair.

- **Ten of Swords** – Woe is me attitude, negativity, inner struggle, survival.
- **Page of Swords** – Message on a legal or mind level, strategic idea, contracts.
- **Knight of Swords** – Brave action, courageous, hasty, confidence, stirring.
- **Queen of Swords** – Perceptive, truthful, sharp-tongued, honest.
- **King of Swords** – Firm but fair leader, intelligence, authority, honest leader.

Pentacles (Earth)
– Physical world, Finances, Work

- **Ace of Pentacles** – New beginning surrounding physical or material world.
- **Two of Pentacles** – Work-life balance, financial balance, balance of energies.
- **Three of Pentacles** – Teamwork, collaboration, co-operation, building for future.
- **Four of Pentacles** – Holding on too tightly, savings, materialism, keeping ideas private.
- **Five of Pentacles** – Ask for help, loneliness, tightening finances, sometimes ill health.
- **Six of Pentacles** – Generosity, equality, bad spending habits.
- **Seven of Pentacles** – Reflection, evaluation, fresh perspectives, re-assess.
- **Eight of Pentacles** – Hard work, focus, working on your craft.

- **Nine of Pentacles** – Decadence, treats, comfortable, remaining disciplined.
- **Ten of Pentacles** – Alignment, stability, wellbeing, gratitude, legacy.
- **Page of Pentacles** – Message related to goals, opportunity, ideas, material world.
- **Knight of Pentacles** – Hardworking action, dependable, practical, reliable.
- **Queen of Pentacles** – Stability, simplicity, growth, sanctuary, nurturing.
- **King of Pentacles** – Material dreams emerging, fulfilment, willing, hard-working leader.

CHAPTER ELEVEN

The Court Cards

As part of the Rider Waite Smith tarot deck there are traditionally four suits: cups, swords, pentacles and wands. Each suit will have a Page, Knight, Queen and King. In other decks they may have name variations, such as coins for pentacles, but will follow a similar pattern. When these characters appear in a reading, they usually represent either the client or another person in the client's life - whether they have appeared yet or not but how can we decipher who they might be? By looking at the elements they represent and the associated sun signs, we may get some clues.

- **Wands** - characters are ruled by fire. This means they are more likely to be an Aries, Leo or Sagittarius.
- **Cups** - are ruled by water and so may be someone with the star sign Cancer, Scorpio or Pisces.
- **Swords -** are ruled by air. This would indicate they may be a Gemini, Libra or Aquarius.
- **Pentacles -** are ruled by the earth. This would be zodiac signs Taurus, Virgo or Capricorn.

For example, if the Queen of Swords is pulled alongside The Sun card, you could look to the air signs Gemini, Libra or Aquarius for clues as to who they might be. With The Sun card, it would certainly indicate there will be a lot of joy and happiness coming either from this person or for this person.

Please note that whilst the Rider Waite Smith deck is based on keywords, which are quite gender specific in their images and character titles, the Queens do not always have to be women. They could be a male with these characteristics. Many modern decks are now much more diverse, both in their representation of images and titles.

CHAPTER TWELVE

Tarot Cards and Astrology Signs

The Fool
The Fool is associated with the planet Uranus, which is the planet of freedom, rebellion. They are both motivated by change and new beginnings. They are also both considered to be a little eccentric. The Fool card represents taking a leap of faith and trusting in the universe and the idea that action is the way forwards.

The Magician
The Magician is linked to the planet Mercury. The Magician uses the power of the mind to manifest the reality he dreams of. He is proof that our thoughts really can shape our world. In most cards where there is a figure, he is pictured with one arm up and one down representing *'as above, so below,'* linking the spiritual world with the physical world. I think this is important when tapping into why tarot and astrology are such useful tools, linking our world and the powers greater than us.

The High Priestess

The Moon rules the night and is linked with The High Priestess in tarot. Many tarot readers and other spiritual people, recognise themselves as The High Priestess as she is a mystic who can see between this world and the next using whatever tools are necessary. The High Priestess embodies the Moon with her intuition and reflection.

The Empress

The Empress is associated with the planet Venus; in fact it is almost as though the planet Venus has taken on a kind of human form in many tarot decks for this card. She is often illustrated as pregnant and is a symbol of fertility and growth, whether this is the birth of a child or the birth of new projects and passions. Both Venus and The Empress share a love of beauty. Creativity is also linked here, with love also being a powerful force of creation.

The Emperor

The Emperor card is related to the sign of Aries as the leader of the zodiac signs. Aries is associated with being fearless, confident and courageous as is The Emperor. He is always ready to defend his realm and is adventurous and decisive, forceful and knows where his boundaries lie. He is clear on what he will accept and what he won't.

The Hierophant

The Hierophant is a card associated with traditional structures and is linked to Taurus. Taurus is a sign of stability and convention, as is the Hierophant character. The Hierophant is the final authority on matters of faith, serving as a bridge between this world and the next. The Hierophant is also often known as a teacher, healer or a counsellor of some sort.

The Lovers

The Lovers card depicts twins who share a wide range of thoughts and experiences. This card is associated with Gemini, which is known as the great communicator of the zodiac. Gemini is also linked to the idea of twins. Whilst The Lovers card can be linked to romance, it is also about like-minded spirits who can discuss and speak freely with each other.

The Chariot

The Chariot card is linked to the zodiac sign of Cancer. Cancer is very much linked to the home and family. Whilst it may seem strange for this sign to be connected to The Chariot, The Chariot takes a little piece of home with him on his adventures. In fact, he seems to actually ride in a Chariot that looks like a small home. Adventures are usually related to making a better life for Cancer zodiac sun signs.

Strength

The Strength card is about bravery and the inner knowing that you are stronger than any challenges before you. Strength is related to the zodiac sign of Leo as they are known to be warm, generous, strong-minded, honourable and energetic. People who are Leo are also usually quite proud, just like the figure on the card.

The Hermit

The Hermit likes to keep watch over the world in his hermit cave, holding universal wisdom within him. He is linked to the sign of Virgo, which is the sign of duty and service to others. Both The Hermit and Virgos are typically conscientious, self-disciplined and reliable, although they can be perfectionists. The Hermit traditionally carries a lantern containing an eight-pointed star, a symbol for following his own inner wisdom.

Wheel Of Fortune

The expansive planet of Jupiter, the bringer of luck and good fortune, is associated with the Wheel of Fortune. Jupiter will grow all it has contact with. Most versions of the Wheel of Fortune depict some form of a spinning wheel. The trick with this card is remaining resilient while more prosperous changes come in on the wind. Both the card and the planet represent luck, opportunity and fate playing a part in what is to come.

Justice
The Justice card is linked to the sign of Libra. Usually the Justice card is pictured with balance scales, which is used as the symbol of Libra linking both of them to balance, equality and grace. Librans are often good at problem solving and finding diplomatic solutions and the Justice card, highlights the importance of honesty and truth.

The Hanged Man
The Hanged Man spends a long time hanging around (!) and so is the perfect partner to Neptune, the planet of spiritual enlightenment. It is also known as the psychic planet. Neptune is made up mostly of ethereal mist and gases and is a dreamy planet. Both The Hanged Man and Neptune are linked to imagination, fantasy and psychic abilities. If the Hanged Man appears in a tarot reading it can indicate a need to retreat within.

Death
Many people fear the Death card but it is actually a card of transition and change. The Death card is related to the sign of Scorpio, which is known for being unafraid of the *'dark.'* Scorpios know that Death does not always come with the sting in their Scorpio tails. In a reading, the Death card signifies the end of one chapter and the start of another, a whole new phase in your life.

Temperance

The Temperance card usually depicts some kind of alchemy taking place where the journey is just as important as the final success. It is linked to the sign of Sagittarius which is a sign associated with long-distance travel, higher education and philosophy. For Sagittarians, the journey is more important than a final destination, making them the perfect duo with the Temperance card.

The Devil

The Devil card is associated with the sign of Capricorn. The Devil card energy can involve a preoccupation with materialism, something Capricorns understand the temptations of. Both this card and the zodiac sign share an important feature of understanding the temptations in the material world. People with this sun sign are usually hard-workers and high achievers, often leading in business in some way. The Devil gives us an insight into the darker side of this with greed, envy, pride and perhaps power struggles.

The Tower

The Tower is related to the warrior planet of Mars. Mars is linked to our drive, ambition and also how we treat our enemies. The Tower is often depicted as being under attack by all the elements. Both The Tower and Mars symbolise quick and sudden bursts of energy. Often, The Tower can bring a bolt from the blue. However, this is not always bad energy, it perhaps could be bringing about inspiration or marking the start of a life change.

The Star

The Star card is linked to the sign of Aquarius, which is an innovative sign and one that likes to be original. Aquarians are usually freethinking and can be a little eccentric. For years, the stars have been used as a tool to help storytelling and for describing our hopes and dreams. The stars give these freethinking Aquarians some centred direction.

The Moon

Pisces is usually connected to intuition and known for being one of the most spiritual signs of the zodiac. Pisces is a sensitive, compassionate and intuitive sign, just like moon energy. Its shadow side can, however, be restless, self-destructive and quite secretive. The Moon reveals itself in phases with only a few days in a lunar cycle where we see the whole picture. The Moon card meaning draws on these similarities in a reading.

The Sun

The Sun is an important point of astrology birth charts, representing the self. In tarot, it is no surprise to find The Sun card associated with the sun itself, suggesting vitality, energy and strength. It also represents our consciousness and how we identify as ourselves. Many tarot decks picture a beautiful child who is said to be the Greek and Roman god Apollo. Apollo was a God of healing and of light.

Judgment

Pluto is the planet of transformation and is linked to the Judgment card. Most versions of the Judgment card depict people being reborn, with this card associated with positive transformations towards a higher purpose. It is a card also connected to following your inner knowing and in turn, your true path. Both the Judgment card and Pluto teach us that endings are just part of a cycle before rebirth.

The World

Both The World and Saturn have clearly defined boundaries, with Saturn being the planet of restrictions and The World following scientific laws and physics. Saturn's association with The World card identifies that wise people make the most of the time and resources they've been given to achieve success. Saturn is also a planet of discipline, often much needed for the achievement of goals suggested by The World card.

CHAPTER THIRTEEN

Key To The Tarot Symbols

The following symbols are based around the Rider Waite Smith tarot deck.

Angels
Angels represent the potential for the involvement of divine intervention in a situation. The angels will support you if they appear and they will be working on a situation behind the scenes. The angel traditionally in The Lovers card is thought to be Archangel Raphael looking over those searching for a soul mate.

Cats
Cats, in particular black cats, have long been associated with magical powers. They are also known as very savvy keepers of secrets. Cats are generally related to having ultimate authority over their inner realm. The black cat in the Queen of Wands represents how comfortable the queen is with herself as she is seen with, what was in 1909, a controversial symbol.

Chains

We can see chains in The Devil card and in tarot they represent self-limiting behaviour. This could be anything from too much junk food to something worse. There are certainly bonds to something that is not really serving you in The Devil card.

Circles

Circles can often represent cycles or things that are evolving. In the case of the King of Wands or The World card, there is also an element of completion and of achievement.

Dogs

Dogs in tarot are usually associated with themes of communication, friendship and community. They can also represent protection or some kind of guardian or support by your side. They are generally considered auspicious signs.

Falcons

In the Nine of Pentacles we see a lady with a falcon. Falcons have a high intellect and can be highly focused. They have a high ability to hone in on their targets. This falcon represents, that we ourselves have focused on very specific goals. The result of this is abundance.

Fish

On a simple level, a fish jumping out of a cup, as seen in the Page of Cups, is quite a surprising event!

Therefore, it can represent pleasant and surprising news, particularly associated with emotions. On another level, it can be a symbol of going with the flow or accessing a deeper subconscious level of thought.

Caduceus

The caduceus symbol, pictured in the Two of Cups is related to health and healing and is often used in the medical profession. The Two of Cups is, after all, about a union or re-union and healing as part of this.

Infinity Loop

The infinity Symbol, or lemniscate, means adored with ribbons. It is a geometrical representation of the continuing motion of energy and matter, reminding us to remain present, conscious of where we are and the endless possibilities before us. In its simplest form, it represents balance - particularly between the physical and spiritual worlds.

Keys

Keys can represent some kind of liberation from a situation. They can also be interpreted as providing access to a hidden secret. In the Hierophant card we see two figures and two keys approaching the Hierophant. This would indicate they hold the key themselves to the answers they seek.

Lobster or Crayfish

In The Moon card we can see a lobster emerging from the water. This represents us emerging from more *'animal'* thinking into our divine potential. It can represent the start of a journey to a higher purpose. Crabs have a link to the astrological sign of Cancer, with the moon as its planetary ruler.

Rabbits

Rabbits can bear up to 5 litters a year, each producing 3-6 bunnies. It is, therefore, no surprise that rabbits in tarot are often associated with fertility. They are also sometimes linked to life cycles, lunar energies and lively antics!

Sphinx

The two sphinxes in The Chariot represent opposition with their black and white colours. They represent external forces that need to be managed, in order for victory to be achieved. The sphinxes need to go in one joint direction for the battle to be won or for success to be achieved.

Tree of Life Formation

The tree of life in its entirety, represents the universe on all levels of consciousness. This includes physical, subconscious, emotional, intellectual and spiritual levels. The first known example of this originates in Turkey from 7000BC. In Kabbalah it is believed to be a representation of how the universe came into existence. The Ten of Pentacles, which depicts the tree of life, is a card of fulfilment and *'wealth'* in all areas of life.

Wreath

Generally, the appearance of a wreath represents victory and accomplishments. Often associated with the God Apollo, it is a sign that the favour of the Gods is upon you and that you shall be the victor at this point in your life.

CHAPTER FOURTEEN

To Infinity and Beyond!

The infinity symbol is often used in modern day jewellery designs, tattoos and artwork and appears in the Rider Waite Smith tarot deck. The symbol was *'discovered'* as a mathematical device in 1655 by John Wallis but its religious connotations go back much further, originating in Arabic numerals.

There are four cards in the Rider Waite Smith tarot deck that have the infinity symbol pictured. These are The Magician, Strength, The World and the Two of Pentacles. Whilst they are quite visible in The Magician, Strength and the Two of Pentacles, the symbol is slightly subtler in The World card.

The Magician has the infinity symbol clearly displayed above his head and we can see all *'suits'* of the Rider Waite Smith deck represented with a cup, pentacle, sword and wand. This represents he has all he needs for manifesting and the infinity sign further adds to this. It is a sign that he also has a connection to the universe and can use the power of the divine to create the world of his choice. The never ending loop in this card shows us he is connected to both the physical and the spiritual worlds, is in balance and is ready to begin his journey.

The Strength card also clearly depicts the infinity loop above the figure's head. Whilst The Magician uses his connection to the divine for manifesting, the figure in The Strength card uses it for spiritual strength. It allows the figure to have the right force at the right time for balancing their world and is taming the lion with gentleness and compassion. This inner strength, will allow the figure to demonstrate bravery and endurance during the journey ahead. They are stronger than all challenges ahead of them.

The World card also contains two infinity symbols but can you spot them? They are depicted as red ribbons looped around the wreath, perhaps taking on the very literal meaning of *'lemniscate.'* In this card, they signify that the connection to infinite wisdom is part of the whole being. It represents a state of oneness and being present in the moment. The dancer has achieved perfect balance, floating between the heavens and Earth, surrounded by symbols that represent the four elements. With one step through the wreath the figure will soon begin a journey.

The final card containing an infinity symbol is the Two of Pentacles. Here, a figure is clearly juggling two pentacles, contained within an infinity loop representing the physical or material world in some way. The figure is desperately trying to keep everything in balance, even with one foot off the ground. This card is showing us that balancing the realities of the physical world is achievable but reminds us, that we do need to look at the bigger picture with regard to balance in our lives. By allowing the flow of life to keep going through the infinity loop, the figure can juggle both opposing forces.

Tarot cards are rich with symbolism and these signs may differ between decks. You may find the infinity loop in many other cards of different deck designs, representing slightly different things depending on their context. It is always worth looking into any symbols you are unsure of when reading tarot for yourself and others.

CHAPTER FIFTEEN

Numerology in Tarot

It is commonly thought that it was the Arabic people who devised numbers as we know them today, although there are also claims that ancient Hindu writings acquired the knowledge from the Gods. The Chinese took these numbers further, for example attributing qualities such as fire to some numbers and the colour white to odd numbers. These attributes were used later by Pythagoras in his system in the 6th century BC, believing the movement of planets, seasons and human actions could be quantified into mathematical laws. During the 18th Century, a numerological system was devised that was heavily based on what was known of Kabbalah by Henry Agrippa. This involved converting a person's name into numbers. As the early 20th Century began, Count Louis Hamon (Cheiro) was one of the most renowned numerologists, as well as being a palm reader. He worked with numbers and the nobility, making numerology much more commonly recognised.

Whilst the Aces are not a number in themselves, they are the start of each suit as there is no number 1 in the tarot. Aces are new beginnings and are that sudden flash of inspiration that either comes to you, is offered to you, or sometimes forced upon you. What area of your life this new beginning falls in will depend on the suit so look to those for further guidance.

The number 2 is all about choice and balance. There are cards depicting happy unions or reunions with the 2's but also cards depicting a need for balance or a certain duality regarding an upcoming choice. The surrounding cards will also give hints as to which is appropriate. In the Two of Swords in the Rider Waite Smith deck, we see a figure blindfolded, not looking at the choices in front of them compared to the Two of Wands, where planning can be done to broaden horizons and widen choices.

The number 3 has a certain mystical quality about it. Folk-tales include many 3's, whether they are 3 wishes or 3 sisters. It appears in Christianity with the Holy Trinity, the Father, Son and Holy Ghost. It is connected to growth and creativity but can also bring chaos with it. After all, not all growth is comfortable. The Three of Cups is a particularly celebratory 3, with 3 figures dancing and celebrating an abundant harvest.

The number 4 in tarot is associated with structure, stability and sometimes rest. It is a time to take a pause and ensure all things are stable around you. Following the 3, it is a card where more balance is established and where commitments are firm and faithful. The Four of Wands can sometimes signal an upcoming marriage with the link to commitment.

The 5's are trickier cards in the tarot and often represent a conflict, either in your outer or inner life. They can also represent forced growth and the need for adaptability. The Five of Pentacles, can be particularly daunting with two figures literally out in the cold. The key to the 5's is to take refuge and be open to receive help where it is needed when these cards appear.

Following the trickier 5's, the number 6 is a card related to more harmonious times. It is associated with success, having tackled the conflicts of the 5's and is often related to beauty. In astrology, the number 6 is linked to the planet Venus, the goddess of love. It is no surprise then that it can sometimes bring love and partnerships and of course, could also be related to friendships or business too. The 6's can also bring lots of happiness through hard work.

In myths, the number 7 is often associated with sleep and peace. In Christianity, God created the world in 6 days, resting on the 7th. Our universe is also full of 7's with the days of the week or colours of the rainbow. It is considered a magical number often associated with the unconscious mind. In tarot, the 7's are about strategies, planning and sometimes being cunning to achieve victory. The Seven of Cups is an interesting card of illusion, where multiple choices are presented but all is not what it seems.

The number 8 is always related to strength, change and release. In fact, the number 8 card in the Rider Waite Smith Major Arcana is usually called Strength and if you turn the number on its side it becomes an infinity symbol. The number 8 brings with it wisdom and patience, tackling any challenges. The Eight of Wands is the only card without a figure on it and can represent strong and quick progress.

The last single digit number of the tarot deck is the number 9. The 9's in the tarot are associated with contentment, reflection and evaluation for all that has gone before. The Nine of Cups in particular is one of the *'wish'* cards, with your heart's desires on the way.

The last numbered card in the suits are the 10's. The number 10 in tarot is associated with fulfilment, completion and is the pinnacle of the number sequence in the suits. The number 10 reduces back down to 1 (10=1+0=1) and so starts the number sequence off again. Often, when 10's appear we have made great achievements or have all we need in order to start a new journey or move forward to a new phase in our lives.

This quick guide to numerology in the tarot should help you to look beyond the suits and pictures on cards, and also look for numbers and patterns within them.

CHAPTER SIXTEEN

The Fool's Journey

You may have heard the term *'The Fool's journey'* before but not been completely clear on what exactly that was referring to. The Fool's journey involves all of the Major Arcana cards numbered from 0 – 21. Major Arcana cards are great spiritual lessons, things we need to learn and various forces of nature we might have to meet on a journey. Every one of them asks you to delve into its mysteries so you can welcome the mysteries in life. They are the secrets that we will encounter on our life's journey. The Fool card is at the start of this journey, learning and growing as he moves through each Major Arcana card in order whilst on his path.

Each Major Arcana card represents a stage on his journey. If you look at The Fool card in the Rider Waite Smith deck, he has a knapsack that he carries on a wand. That wand symbolises magic and the knapsack is filled with not only his past experiences but also the tools he needs to move forwards, with total confidence. Now we're not talking about nails, wood and drills but the more spiritual tools such as tarot, meditation, affirmations or ceremonial magic. It is a journey of personal growth and enlightenment.

Many approaches break down The Fool's journey into three horizontal rows of 7, with The Fool being separate as he is the one undertaking the journey. This is loosely based on Plato's theory of the soul being divided into three parts, the soul of desire, the soul of will and the soul of reason. Cards 1 – 7 make up the first row, cards 8 – 14 make up the second row and cards 15 – 21 are the last row. Cards 1 – 7 represent our conscious, cards 8 – 14 how we develop certain qualities and our subconscious, with cards 15 – 21 showing us that prioritising material matters will not bring us nearer to our inner goals with our spiritual awareness. The final card, The World, represents accomplishments with old patterns being released, replaced with new ones. The Fool is moving towards a higher truth and the journey begins again.

The cards on this journey can, of course, be read individually with regard to a person or situation but it is always useful to keep in mind their part in The Fool's journey. Each card is an integral part of a process and can give an indicator how far along someone is on a journey, or in dealing with a situation.

CHAPTER SEVENTEEN

Smoke Cleansing

Cleansing using plant leaves is a Native American tradition of the Sacred Smoke Blow Blessing and is a powerful cleansing technique calling on sacred plants to drive away negative energies. It is a very simple process and doesn't require lots of expensive equipment. In fact, you can even make your own cleansing sticks. Smoke cleansing allows you to wash away any emotional or spiritual negative energy that might gather in your home or body over time. In the case of tarot, it cleanses the deck of the energies focused on throughout a reading, leaving it fresh for use again. Originally, herbs and resins were placed in a special bowl and burned but cleansing sticks allow for an easy and portable way for cleansing to take place. How often you decide to cleanse your deck is entirely up to you. Go with what you feel works best. As a professional tarot reader, I always cleanse my decks in some way before and after a reading. This ensures my energy doesn't influence the reading and clears energy from any previous clients.

In order to smoke cleanse your deck you are going to need a cleansing stick. These can be bought at many good spiritual shops. White sage is commonly found in cleansing sticks as it is said to bring peace and harmony and is often used to cleanse tarot decks. Native Americans often used it to cleanse their ritual tools. Cleansing sticks can, however, contain a range of leaves or flowers depending on their focus. Blue Sage and Mistletoe are great for attracting love, health, fertility and for protection. For winter cleansing fir, holly or pine are sometimes added for purifying benefits.

You can also make your own smoke cleansing sticks. These can be just as effective in cleansing yourself, your home and tarot decks. Making your own cleansing sticks is relatively easy to do and you can use flowers, plants and leaves from your own garden to give it a personal touch. You can also hold in your mind, during the making process or during a meditation, a specific intention for the cleansing stick, allowing it to focus on a particular benefit.

But how do I smoke cleanse my deck?

The cleansing process is very simple. Once you have your cleansing stick you will need some kind of small bowl or tray to catch the ash. Then simply light the end - I use a candle lighter - and within a few seconds a small thread of smoke will begin to weave up from the stick. Once you are happy with the level of smoke you can pass your tarot deck through the smoke several times, as you feel appropriate and it is cleansed. When cleansing yourself or your home, you may like to use a traditional large feather to waft the smoke over yourself or into the corners of rooms to thoroughly cleanse areas. Don't forget to open the windows to allow any negativity to pass out.

Palo Santo is another option when wanting to cleanse a tarot deck. Palo Santo is a stick of wood from the tree Bursera Graveolens, that grows in South America. Palo Santo, when translated, is called Holy Wood and the smoke that comes from burning it comes from an Incan tradition. South American Shamans believe Palo Santo has similar cleansing abilities to sage.

Whether you are using cleansing sticks or Palo Santo, you might also like to use a shell of some kind to gather the ashes. Abalone shells are often used to collect any hot cinders or as a place to put any cleansing tools when they are hot. Abalone shells are said to bring feelings of peace and open up our intuitive side.

With all smoke cleansing, please be extremely careful. Ensure you have somewhere you can let the ashes fall, whether that be into a shell, dish or other receptacle.

CHAPTER EIGHTEEN

Tarot Myths

As a tarot reader I have heard many myths about the tarot from a range of people. This section is about dispelling the myths and the fear surrounding receiving a tarot reading.

1. The Death card means you are going to die! Absolutely not! It merely means change is on the way. It could be a change of job, the end of a relationship and new love coming in or simply a new, more confident, you. A tarot reader will definitely not predict your impending doom with any cards.
2. Tarot cards are the work of the devil. Again, this myth is not true. Tarot readers aim to help their clients, giving them guidance and enabling them to make clearer decisions in their lives.
3. Tarot readers are not to be trusted. Always choose a reader who you feel comfortable with and trust your intuition on this. In every profession you will find people you can't trust but don't assume all tarot readers are like this. Tarot readers come from all walks of life

and many tarot readers are also professional business people. They may be doctors, nurses, scientists or teachers alongside being a reader.

4. Tarot cards are always right. A good reader will reveal your future possibilities but the reality depends on you. This is why I always say the final card or cards in a general spread show a potential future. You always have freedom of choice and can change your circumstances should you wish.

5. You can't buy your own tarot cards they must be gifted. If this was true, I would never have learnt to read tarot! It is important to choose your own cards as you can allow your intuition to steer you towards a deck most suited to you. I have some decks I have been gifted, some I have chosen and one special deck that I primarily use that has followed me most of my life.

6. Tarot cards must be wrapped in silk. False. You can store cards however you choose and however feels best for you. I like to keep my main deck in a wooden box with crystals that I know are known for protection. However, some of my decks remain in their original boxes and work just as well.

7. You can't receive a reading over the phone, internet or via email. As long as the reader is

focused on that client throughout shuffling and pulling of cards, the results remain the same. My email readings are just as accurate as my face-to-face readings. With face-to-face readings, there may be more flexibility where clients can ask questions or spend longer delving into one particular question.

8. Tarot cards are magical. The images or signals in the cards can spark clues as to the client's life or potential future. An intuitive reader can see these and advise accordingly. The cards themselves are often mass-produced and are not *'magical'* but readers can build up strong relationships with decks through cleansing them, sleeping with them under their pillow, through continual work with them or through other rituals.

9. Tarot decks don't reflect real people's identities, backgrounds, and lives. It is true that pictorially some of the most popular decks from the last 100 years seem only representative of certain kinds of people such as slim, able-bodied, straight, white people. This is now changing and has certainly picked up pace in the last few years with many more diverse decks becoming available. A good reader will be able to put aside these differences when reading and look at the character

of a card. They will focus on the qualities this card brings as opposed to attaching it to a specific gender or background, for example.
10. Tarot decks should not be touched by lots of people. This is based on the assumption that *'imprints'* of energy will be left on the cards. This can actually be very useful when reading for others as an energy exchange can take place, allowing information to flow more easily. A skilled tarot reader, will be able to cleanse their deck easily between client readings, should they feel any scrambling of energy has taken place.

CHAPTER NINETEEN

The Good Guys

Whilst all cards do have positive and negative aspects, particularly if you read reversals of cards, these are some cards that generally bring joy and happiness to me when I see them jump out.

The Sun. A card of joy, happiness and contentment. This is my and many others', favourite card in the Rider Waite Smith deck. Traditionally, it shows blazing sunshine beaming over a naked child on a white horse. Many decks take inspiration from this image. The sun card speaks of the joy of childish abandon, having few cares in the world and feeling a true sense of happiness. If you are having difficulties in any areas in life and this card appears, you can be certain that much better times lie ahead.

The Empress is the epitome of Mother Nature with the Rider Waite Smith deck picturing an abundant harvest surrounding her. She is a strong, matriarchal character who can make any idea or project fruitful. She can also represent fertility, appearing often when there is a pregnancy, or just when matters are going to produce a good harvest for a client. She is also associated with luxury and beauty and all that is linked with pleasure. Should a client be asking about a career, if the Empress turns up, the job will surely bring success, abundance and all things related to luxury.

The Star card traditionally contains a lot of symbolism but is largely related to wishes coming true and it being your time to shine. On the card, many eight-pointed stars are pictured. Numerically, the number eight is largely associated with strength, suggesting you do have what it takes to fulfil what it is you dream of. The Star also depicts the figure pouring from two jugs of water. One jug represents her subconscious and one her conscious. Traditionally, she pours one into the water to nourish the earth and another on to dry land into five streams, representing the five senses being nourished. The Star card always brings renewed hope, faith and a sense of peace.

The Magician. Lastly I come to the Magician. In this card, we see all four suits in the tarot represented; a cup, a sword, a wand and a pentacle. The Magician is all about manifesting and using all that you have to do this. Having all four suits represented suggests that all elements are working together towards achieving a common goal. How you manifest what you would like is up to you. This could be materially, using all the skills and resources you have in the material world in unison for success. Or, it could be on a much more spiritual level, using all four elements to go within, manifesting and asking the universe to support you in your journey. However you approach things, the Magician has a strong divine connection contributing to achievements.

Whilst there are many other cards that can bring great things into our lives, such as The World and The Wheel of Fortune, these are four of my favourite cards. Which one's appeal most to you?

CHAPTER TWENTY

The Scary Cards

On the flip side of this there are always some cards that are more dreaded. A reading could be looking pretty good and then you pull a card and out pops the Tower! It's quite hard not to get sucked into the instant reaction of fear and thinking the worst is about to happen.

The Tower depicts a scene of chaos with bodies flying from a burning building as lightning strikes it. I'll admit on first glance, it doesn't look too good. However, we have all had our *'Tower'* moments ranging from finally leaving that job we hate, to a house sale falling through only for us to go on to find the home of our dreams. The Tower is a great clearer of old energy and of things that are no longer serving us. It may come as a bolt from the blue and may certainly bring some drastic changes to your life. These changes are going to be needed though for things to keep moving forwards. The Tower, although feeling destructive at times, clears the old out and makes room and space for the new to come in. I like to pull a clarifying card alongside The Tower to try and decipher in what area of life a client may be about to experience some *'Tower'* energy, which often helps to put this card into perspective and gives more insight into where major changes are needed, or coming. Sometimes this energy may be positive, with The Tower brining sudden pleasant changes too. Surrounding cards will give you a clue.

The Death card is another card that strikes fear into the hearts of clients, but fear not. The Death card is associated with change and after all, there is that lovely golden sun in the background hinting at better things coming on the horizon. If things have been tricky recently, the Death card may be a very positive card, showing an end to this period. New phases are certainly on their way when the Death card is around and may actually prove to be much more prosperous times than recent events in a client's life.

The Devil card is not the most inviting of cards but is often quite misunderstood in the Rider Waite Smith deck. Whilst it may look like he has the two figures chained up below him, their chains are actually rather loose and could probably be removed, should they choose to; this is the key to this card. When it appears in a spread it often represents our shadow side, which we all have and self-indulgence, possibly too much chocolate or wine, or something far more self-destructive. There is power in this card in that you can choose to unchain yourself.

Lastly I come to The Hanged Man whose name is actually quite deceiving in that he is not hanging by his neck from a noose but by his ankle. When The Hanged Man is around, nothing is going to happen quickly and there may be a lot of *'hanging around'* going on. The Hanged Man is about accepting where you are at a given time and being present with that. He almost seems to be in a yoga pose suggesting it is a time of meditation, yoga and working on yourself as things perhaps unfold behind the scenes. Again, should The Hanged Man appear in a reading, your impending doom has not been predicted!

Hopefully, this has gone some way to relieving your fears when dealing with these four cards. They are often the ones clients recoil at when I am doing readings for them. Look at them with fresh eyes next time you have a tarot reading.

CHAPTER TWENTYONE

The Questions We All Want Answered

As I read for more and more clients, I began to see similar themes appearing in their concerns. Whilst there may have been different circumstances surrounding every reading, themes of questions were largely based on career, romance, travel or movement, fertility or some way of finding out if a deep desire was going to come into fruition. This chapter will identify some of the cards associated with these themes. It is by no means an exhaustive list and when other tarot cards are combined in pairs, or more, they too may display similar meanings. These are just some of the cards to watch out for regarding signs surrounding these topics.

Good signs for Career

When asking about career, whether a current job, a possible promotion or when looking for employment, these are always great cards to see. The Six of Wands is a card of success and victory, with victory wreaths worn by the figure and appearing on what seems to be a jousting stick. There is certainly someone pictured receiving lots of glory so if this appears for you, things are looking good. There is recognition and reward in this card. Alongside this, the Ace of Wands is a good omen. Aces are new beginnings and wands are associated with your energy, ambition, passions and perhaps projects too. If you are looking for a promotion, new job or wanting to start your own business, this is a very positive card to see. Due to the hand positioning on it, it's sometimes nicknamed the *'thumbs up'* card. The King of Pentacles is related to abundance in the physical world, which can include finances. If you're hoping for a pay rise, you might just be lucky if this card appears in a spread. The King of Wands is a passionate, enthusiastic and inspiring leader who has many great accomplishments. This card might arise if it's time to move up the career ladder, perhaps taking more of a management role. I would also include The Magician with these cards as he is so good at manifesting and creating the life he wants using all tools available to him. He could, in fact, be related to any of the themes and is usually a positive influence.

Relationships and Romance

When having a tarot reading, we often like to receive guidance surrounding our relationships which could be in a romantic way, with family, colleagues or may actually be about self-love. The Four of Wands is a card of commitment and more structure and stability coming into your life. This card, therefore, can sometimes be related to a forthcoming engagement or wedding when asking about relationships. The Page of Cups usually brings pleasant and surprising news, particularly regarding our emotions and feelings, which could be an offering of love and support or a new love appearing in your life. The Knight of Cups, incidentally can also be a real Romeo of the tarot. The Ace of Cups could indicate a new relationship starting or a new loving and peaceful period beginning emotionally. It may also be an offering with that open hand placement. The last card I would highlight is The Lovers card. The appearance of this card does not mean that a new love is instantly on the way, as its impression gives, but rather is a card for creating more harmonious relationships in your life. There could also be several options available to you when pulling The Lovers card.

Travel or Movement

Often it's nice to find out if we're going off on holiday soon, or if any kind of travel is on the cards. I've also used the word *'movement'* in the header for these cards, as they can also apply to things such as house moves or more spiritual journeys. The World is a good card to see if you'd like to travel in some way. All the elements are working together for achievement in this card and it's also a great card to see with regard to success. The Chariot is a strong card of movement, albeit possibly involving having to navigate some choppy waters in order to get there. This could apply to all areas of travel or movement in some way. The Two and Three of Wands are also indicators that perhaps movement or travel could be on the way. Whilst the Two of Wands is a card of broadening horizons and putting some planning in place for journeys, the Three of Wands is where that journey can start more confidently.

Fertility

Sometimes clients like to know about family matters and about whether that area of their life will be expanding. These cards can also relate to fertility in terms of creativity, projects or abundance in some form. The Three of Cups is all about celebration, abundance and the sharing of accomplishments with others. It is a card that speaks of strong feminine influences. The Empress is traditionally known as the pregnancy card, often seen as the primary signifier of this in a spread. She is a real Mother Nature card and again, represents abundance with that bumper crop before her. The Queen of Pentacles is also related to fertility. In the Rider Waite Smith deck, she holds a pentacle at her stomach but in some decks she is actually pictured as pregnant. She has a rabbit beside her, a symbol of fertility and an abundance of flowers and vines surrounding her growing from fertile ground.

Desires and Wishes

Clients can often get in touch for guidance when there is something in their life that they really desire, that is somehow evading them. These three cards often signify that their desires or wishes may be on the way. The Star is a great card for granting wishes. It is your time to shine when The Star appears, with the things you are wishing for coming into fruition. She is also a card of inner strength and using both intuition and the physical world for achieving goals. The Nine of Cups is traditionally known as a *'wish'* card with an almost genie-like character depicted with all his cups lined up. If this card appears in a spread, your wishes may be about to be granted. The last card is the Ten of Cups and whilst this is not as obviously related to wishes, it is a card of contentment and having all that you need. It may not be what you originally wished for but it could be even better.

All cards have their positives and negatives and many cards' meanings are adjusted when combined with others. These are just some of the quick indicators you can look for if pulling some cards for yourself. Lots will depend on the nature of the question.

CHAPTER TWENTYTWO

Tarot for Your Year Ahead

Finding out your tarot card for your year ahead is simple. All you need to do is add the day and month you were born to the current year. For example:

16th January - 16 + 1 + 2021 = 2038
Then add together the individual numbers in 2038 - 2 +
0 + 3 + 8 = 13 Death card.

Only the Major Arcana cards are used, meaning you need to keep the number under 23 (21 cards plus The Fool as card 22). If you get a number larger than 22, just add together the two single digits again to get your final number for the year ahead.

The card you get can be your card for the coming year, or can be the card you have from one birthday to the next. It is up to individual choice whether to count from the start of the year, or from your birthday. An interesting exercise is to look back and see what cards you have had in previous years and what experiences you had. Were there any repeating cards? Did you have repeated experiences in relation to this?

So what card did you get and what does it mean for your year ahead? Take a look at the brief card summaries below to find out.

1. **The Magician** – Make things happen! A time when you can manifest all your desires and have the perseverance to see plans through to success.
2. **The High Priestess** – A time to trust your intuition and inner knowing. Trust in the universe and be patient,
knowing all will unfold as it should, in time.
3. **The Empress** – Strong links to motherhood, or a time when you may be nurturing others. This could also be a time of great creativity and abundance.
4. **The Emperor** – Time to step up and take the lead in your life. A year for important decisions and being clear on your boundaries.
5. **The Hierophant** – A year for great spiritual development and being your own leader. It could also be a year where teaching or studying takes centre stage.
6. **The Lovers** – Relationships may be the focus for this year. There could be big relationship decisions and a need to follow your heart.
7. **The Chariot** – A year to set big goals and when you can overcome obstacles to achievement. You can take control with skill and determination. This can also be a card of

travel or moving home.

8. **Strength** – Inner strength and courage may be needed this year in order to get to where you want to be. You are stronger than any challenges ahead of you and need to stand up for yourself this year.
9. **The Hermit** – A year of retreat and introspection, prioritising your physical and emotional wellbeing will serve you well this year. Give yourself time to weigh up options.
10. **Wheel Of Fortune** – Prosperous changes ahead with this card of luck. Big changes may be on the horizon, with the ending of one cycle and the beginning of a new one.
11. **Justice** – A year where your focus needs to be on balance and harmony. Keep your integrity through all you do and play fairly. This can also be a card of legal matters.
12. **The Hanged Man** – Things may be on hold this year or there might be periods where you are waiting for things to play out. Being in the present will give you new perspectives on things.
13. **Death** – A card of transformation and of letting go of the old to make room for the new. There can be regeneration with this card and the start of new phases.
14. **Temperance** – A period of alchemy ahead and of trying out different things to find the

right path for you. Be patient with this process, creating a healthy balance for you.
15. **The Devil** – Often representing our shadow side, be careful not to be drawn into being too materialistic this year, or over indulging Don't get too stuck in the old ways of doing things, resisting change. Look for the positives in everything you do.
16. **The Tower** – There could be sudden changes coming if you get this card. This could be positive or negative and may actually be an epiphany of sorts, where you gain a completely new opinion on something.
17. **The Star** – It's your time to shine if you get this card. A period of optimism is ahead, with hope and healing. Wishes and heart's desires may start to come to fruition.
18. **The Moon** – You may find yourself being pulled by an unknown desire if you have this card for your year ahead. Remain positive through any changes, as we often can't see all the factors at play with The Moon. A great year to acknowledge and work with the moon cycles.
19. **The Sun** – Contentment, joy and confidence are ahead if you get this card. Enjoy this period in gratitude. You may also see major achievements or goals being fulfilled in the coming year.

20. **Judgement** – A higher calling may be driving you this year if you get this card. There may be choices ahead but know you will find the right path for you. A rebirth could be just around the corner.
21. **The World** – A card of completion and achievement, there is often great success when we see The World card. There may be many possibilities ahead of you, all of which you can be victorious in.
22. **The Fool** – A big new adventure or new beginning awaits this year. You may have to take a leap of faith but you'll have loyal support and all the tools you need for the journey ahead. Focus on that journey, not the destination.

CHAPTER TWENTYTHREE

Colours in Tarot

Chakra is the Sanskrit word attributed to energy points in our body. Its literal translation, means wheel and chakras are the junction points that energy pathways meet at. The pathways actually meet at triangles but chakras are called wheels as they symbolise growth, dynamism and movement. Most people have only heard of the seven chakras running along the spine but there are actually one hundred and fourteen of them in our bodies. When chakras are working at different levels they can produce different qualities in us. Emotional stress and worries can block our chakras and often chakra healing focuses on getting energy flowing well through them, improving our wellbeing. When chakras are activated through meditation, healing, or a practice such as yoga; your connection to the universe around you and yourself improves.

Traditionally, each of the seven chakras is associated with a colour of the rainbow. This does not mean that the chakras themselves are these colours. The colours indicate the relative vibration of the chakras moving from the slowest at the base to the quickest at the top of the head. The colours themselves also carry certain associations in Western culture, such as red being strong and forceful. The seven main chakra colours from bottom to top are red, orange, yellow, green, blue, indigo and violet or white.

Red - Base/Root Chakra – This is the anchor that links us to all living things, our base in the physical world. The colour red is associated with this chakra, it is our life blood. It often represents the passion and life force itself. Some of the associations when we see red in the tarot are:
- Blood as a life-giving substance,
- Action, passion and inspiration,
- Anger, lust and animal urges,
- Strong will,
- Fertility or menstruation.

Orange - Sacral Chakra – This chakra governs sexuality, procreation and creativity at all levels. This chakra affects the flow of all fluids in the body. When balanced, it brings a sense of self-confidence and creativity, with the imagination used constructively. Orange is not seen as widely as red in the Rider Waite Smith tarot. However, some of the associations are:
- Orange mountains – challenge to overcome by will,
- Courage and vitality,
- Wands cards/energy.

When orange is seen, it could represent a situation that will need action and courage.

Yellow – Solar Plexus – The Solar Plexus extracts and stores Prana: this is the energy that permeates all life - where there is Prana, there is life. Each of the chakras is a centre of Prana but it is the solar plexus where it is generated and distributed. It is our place of empowerment. Some of the associations with yellow are:

- Positivity,
- Intellect,
- Highest level of consciousness,
- Confidence and vibrancy,
- Concentration,
- Masculine (Sun).

There is quite often a yellow instead of blue sky in the Rider Waite Smith deck.

Green - Heart Chakra – It is no surprise that this chakra is associated with love and an inner state of compassion. It is connected to personal love but also moves beyond this, associated with the power to love without discrimination. When balanced, there is a genuine ability to give and receive. When we see green it may represent:

- Nature,
- Abundance and growth,
- Balance, peace and harmony,
- Healing and kindness.

Blue - Throat Chakra – The Throat Chakra represents our power to communicate verbally.

This is unique to humans, despite other species developing their own sophisticated way of communicating. It is also associated with inner hearing, not our day-to-day hearing. When balanced, the power of communication and creativity come to life. When we see blue in tarot it may represent:
- Our subconscious (skies/water),
- Introspective frame of mind (blue clothing),
- Truth,
- Feminine (moon),
- Reflection.

Indigo - Third Eye – This chakra centre acts as the third eye when awakened. It is sometimes known as the *'eye of the soul'* bringing all-round vision. It is associated with liberation as it works outside and beyond all constraints. What does it mean when we see the colour indigo?
- Luxury or opulence,
- Psychic energies,
- Mysteries,
- Insight and wisdom,
- Karmic situation,
- Life lesson.

Violet (White) – Crown Chakra – This chakra is represented as a multi-layered lotus of a thousand white petals symbolising cosmic forces. The level of consciousness represented by the awakened crown chakra, is in itself the epitome of achievement for humans when it comes to chakras. It is thought that

as we as humans have become more enlightened, the colour for this chakra has changed from violet to white. The colour violet in the tarot is related to:
- Universal harmony,
- Spirituality,
- Higher paths or higher selves,
- Inspiration,
- Stimulating mind, body and soul.

Other Notable Colours
White:
- Innocence,
- Purity,
- Light of the moon, feminine,
- Cleansing and rebirth,
- White with black - Black and white pillars – feminine receptive (black) and masculine active (white).

Black:
- Mystery,
- Unknown/in the dark.

Grey:
- Stormy weather,
- Gloom,
- Unhappiness.

Pink:
- Enjoyment,
- Sensual pleasure.

Red, Yellow and Blue:
- Primary colours,
- Assigned to the three 'spiritual elements' fire, air and water,
- Fourth element of earth is green,
- Often found in cards that combine all the elements.

Rainbow Colours:
- Abundance,
- Wishes come true,
- Wide variety of resources to draw upon,
- Integration and celebration of this.

Even by using just the colours in tarot, you can pick up on some simple messages.

CHAPTER TWENTYFOUR

Shuffling The Cards

There is no right or wrong way of shuffling tarot cards, it is completely your choice. When I first started tarot reading, despite playing countless card games with my grandparents when I was younger, I was hopeless at shuffling. Initially, I started out by getting comfortable on the floor and literally spreading out the cards everywhere, mixing them all up and putting them back together. As a long-term strategy this probably wasn't going to work, especially when I needed to be at a table. It's another one of those skills where practice makes perfect. The more shuffling I did, the better I became and I now have a range of methods that I use.

The easiest one is to shuffle the cards using the overhand shuffle method. This is where you hold the deck in your left hand (the side closest to heart and linked to intuition) and slide off a small bundle of cards from the top of the deck using your thumb from the right hand to the left. Using this method, I then either wait until a card jumps out with a message, or when I feel ready, put the deck down, cut it with my left hand, put it back together and then spread the cards in a line, ready for picking. I only tend to cut the deck once but I have seen readers cut the deck into three piles and then put it back together from the bottom pile to the top. Likewise, I like to spread out the cards afterwards but you may prefer drawing from the top of the pile for the reading, or if you only want one card, cutting it again to get the card. A handy tip is to always have a peep at the bottom of the deck, particularly if you need some clarification; it sometimes contains a cheeky extra message.

Another popular way of shuffling cards is the riffle shuffle. This is where you cut the deck in half with your left hand, turn them so the shorted ends are facing each other with thumbs inwards and then the thumbs release the cards so they become interwoven with each other. There is actually some research, that suggests in order to fully shuffle the cards in this way, you would need to do this a minimum of six times. If I use this method, I rarely do it six times but have a try and see what works for you. You can also do this shuffle with the longer ends next to each other, interweaving. I haven't yet mastered it this way around.

These are the two most popular methods of shuffling by tarot readers but there are many other ways you can try. Do some research and see what works for you.

CHAPTER TWENTYFIVE

Reversals

I am going to briefly touch on reversals, although if you are completely new to tarot reading I wouldn't recommend looking into this too much when starting out. Some readers use card reversals in readings and some don't. Either way, it is not a sign of your knowledge or professionalism, it is just personal preference. At the time of writing I don't read reversed cards for clients differently to when they are upright as I feel there are enough meanings in the seventy-eight cards alone and that I don't need that extra meaning for each one. That may change in the future though, depending on what I am drawn to doing.

When a card is pulled and it is reversed, you can just turn it upright and continue to read the cards with all of them upright. I like to try and keep them all upright when I'm shuffling anyway. If you do want to read reversals in tarot, be aware that it is not quite as simple as the card just having the opposite meaning. Reversals are more concerned about the energy of the card manifesting in different ways to when it is upright and having slightly different nuances. If you are just beginning to read tarot cards, my advice would be to learn the upright meanings of all the cards first and use these confidently alongside your intuition, before delving into reversals.

CHAPTER TWENTYSIX

Conducting a Reading

Many readers have their own routines and rituals that they like to do before and after a reading. Some of these are more elaborate than others and again, it is very much about personal choice and what will work for you. Sometimes, it is also what is possible at the time, particularly if you are reading for multiple clients one after another. I'm going to share with you my personal routine and what I do to feel that I am ready to read for a client.

Initially, I really like to do a meditation. This is not always lengthy and is sometimes just for a few minutes. I find that by doing a meditation, it clears my mind of anything that has come before that day and puts me into a more peaceful state ready to work with the cards and receive messages. When I don't have the time to do this between clients at the minimum, I take some deep breaths just to ground myself ready to read. Next, I like to have a good cleanse. As I've already mentioned, this is usually using smoke cleaning with sage or Palo Santo. I cleanse myself to clear any energy from the day that might interfere with the messages the tarot wants to share. I also cleanse the deck, or decks, that I am going to be using and cleanse the space that I am working in. Again, if you are in a space where this isn't possible, you could use chime bells to do this. Then, I like to give the cards a good pre-shuffle. The cards may be in an order from a previous reading or just from how they were last collected up, so I give them a good shuffle so they are ready.

I have some tools that I like to use when reading, so I then start preparing those and laying them out. I have a couple of favourite tarot cloths that I like to lay the cards on. Using a cloth, rather than working on a bare surface, ensures that the area is recognized as special or sacred for the reading. I also have a special crystal that I like to have nearby and often hold it in my hand when reading. It is a sodalite crystal that is great for clarity, seeing things truthfully and for intuition. I feel quite connected to this particular crystal and feel lost if I don't have it nearby when reading now. I also wear a unakite pendant for protection. This is not as traditional for protection as black tourmaline but is a perfect example of doing what you feel drawn to. Unakite is linked to transforming negativity to love. It is important to have some kind of protection for your energy otherwise you are going to feel drained quite quickly when reading professionally. You could use a crystal as I do, or may like to visualise yourself protected in some way. I once heard a reiki healer say that she envisaged having butterfly wings, opening them when she was happy to and then visualizing them closing again when she needed to feel protected, or at the end of a session. It can be very individual.

Once I've gone through these steps, I feel as though I am in the right place to conduct a reading. At the end of a tarot session I like to have a good cleanse again. I cleanse myself, the cards, tools and the space. Depending on how I am feeling, I do sometimes meditate again to ground myself. When I first started seeing clients face-to-face, I used to come home and have a salt bath. If I didn't have this bath I used to find it very difficult to settle.

CHAPTER TWENTYSEVEN

Asking Good Questions

Tarot cards are at their best and most insightful when they can fully express themselves within the framework of a good question. Whilst quick yes or no questions are so tempting and something we all succumb to at times, try to avoid closed questions. Open questions using more than one card will give you a more in-depth look at a situation. Below are some examples of good question starters:

- What can I expect from...
- What do I need to know about...
- How can I prepare for ...
- What's the best path for ...

CHAPTER TWENTYEIGHT

Combining Cards

So far, I have predominantly focused on single card meanings. Something I often get asked about is how to start combining cards. When learning how to read tarot, this can often be a stumbling block. Many people can understand and read single card meanings, using their knowledge and intuition but then find it much trickier to work with a few cards or a larger spread. For me, it is about looking at the story the cards are telling you. I already have a strong knowledge foundation of tarot, including the links to astrology, symbols and the numerology involved. When combining cards, I use this alongside the traditional meanings of the cards to begin linking them.

When you add in your intuition and the themes and ideas you are being drawn to with a card, you can gather a combined meaning. For example, I recently read for a lady who got the King of Wands in a position indicating influences coming into her life and the Ace of Wands in the position of what was coming in on a heart level. The King of Wands came first in the reading and I initially suggested this could be an enthusiastic leader, perhaps a boss, who would bring new enthusiasm to her life and guide her to success, particularly regarding something she was passionate about. After all, we are dealing with the element of fire when with the Wands, so I always link those cards to our passions. I briefly suggested it could, of course, be a new love interest and to look out for an optimistic person with sun sign Aries, Leo or Sagittarius. As the spread evolved and that Ace of Wands appeared on a heart level it started to become clearer that the King of Wands, may be less to do with career and more to do with relationships. The Ace of Wands is a real *'thumbs up'* card that always indicates you should go for something. Aces are also new beginnings and yet again it was with the Wands suit. Noticing this combination in the spread indicated to me that a new beginning was on the horizon with that King of Wands character and the fact that the Ace had appeared in the position of the heart clarified in what area of life this King was going to appear. I later found out that the client was single and looking for a relationship so this was great news from her reading.

When combining cards, there are many features you can look at to help give you clues, alongside the traditional meanings. Is there a predominance of certain suits? Are there cards in the same suit that link together, just like in the example I have just given? Remember that the suits are linked to the elements and so can give a general area of life that the reading is focused on. Is there a common number in the spread? For example, maybe there are lots of six's, in which case perhaps more harmony is on the way for the client. Are there lots of court cards indicating there may be many people around the client at the time, which could be good or bad depending on their situation? Are there lots of a particular court cards? For example, many pages may indicate lots of youthful people around the client or children. I once read for a client who had a lot of pages and I found out after the reading that whilst there might be lots of communication or opportunities coming his way, he also worked with children. If there is a dominance of Major Arcana cards, there may be some big themes going on for the client at the time of reading. Major Arcana cards are often areas for growth, so there could also be lots of development coming on a personal level. If there are many Minor Arcana cards it might indicate a quieter period in life for the client. When looking at combining card meanings, use all the clues you can.

CHAPTER TWENTYNINE

Spread Suggestions

I don't think any book surrounding tarot is complete without some tarot spread suggestions. It's always great to explore some old and tested spreads and try out some new ones. In this section, you will find some of my favourite spreads, starting with very simple spreads for beginners and some that involve more cards to further develop your tarot reading.

Past, Present, Future

Past   Present   Future

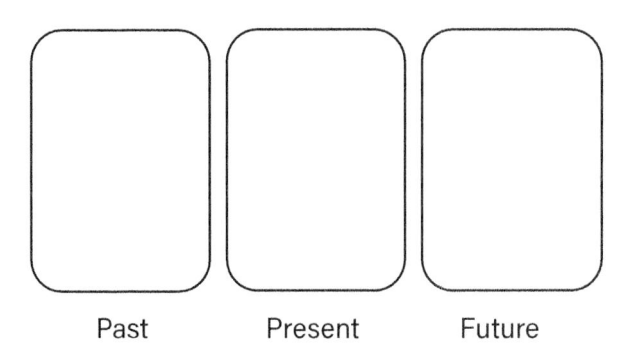

This is a good beginner's spread and one I still do on a weekly basis. The card in the past gives some context for the present situation, with the future card offering insight into what potentially may play out.

Stop, Start, Continue

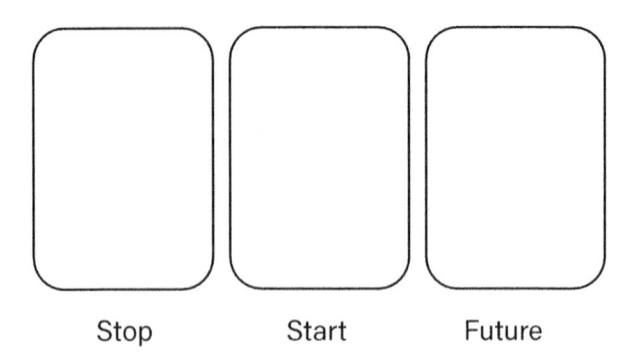

| Stop | Start | Future |

This is another great simple spread, which can be applied to many different situations or questions from clients. It's also good as a general spread. I often use this around once a month, or on a full moon, to reflect on the past month and when making plans for the coming weeks.

Intuition Spread

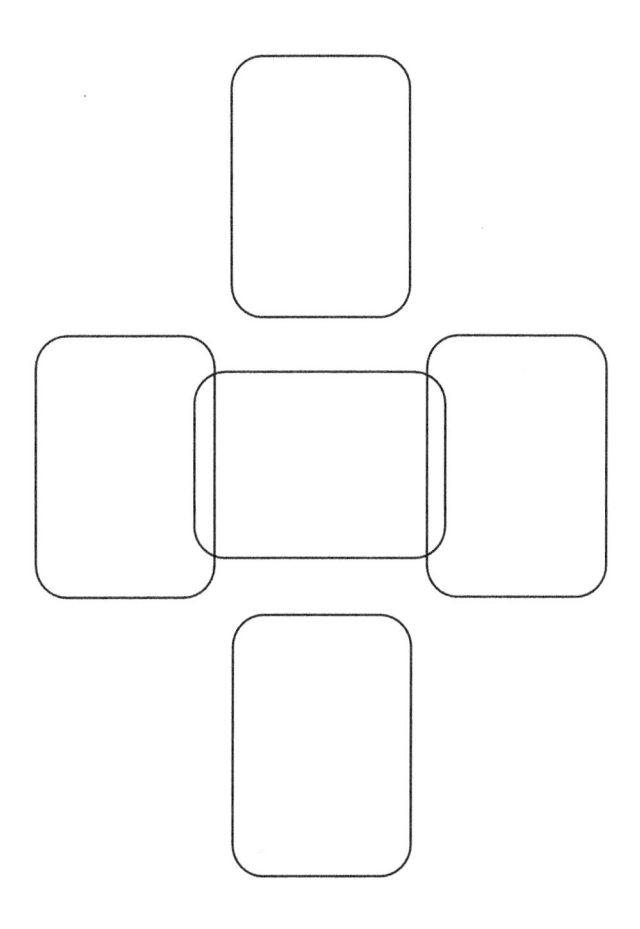

Top – What is at the root of the situation?
Bottom – What can bring clarity?
Middle – Any challenges?
Left – Where can you find support?
Right – What brings balance to the situation?

The Fool's Journey

Top Left – What have you experienced in the past?
Top Middle – What you are experiencing at present?
Top Right – What are you moving into?
Bottom Left – What have you learned from the past?
Bottom Middle – What are you learning now?
Bottom Right – What can you do to stay on your path?

When Things Are Uncertain

Moving clockwise;
Left – What is possible?
Top Left – What have you experienced in the past?
Top Middle – Where do you need to be brave?
Top Right – What is trivial?
Right - What action is needed?
Bottom Right – Where can you find support?
Bottom Middle – Where might challenges occur?
Bottom Left – What can help you move forwards?

The Horse Shoe Spread

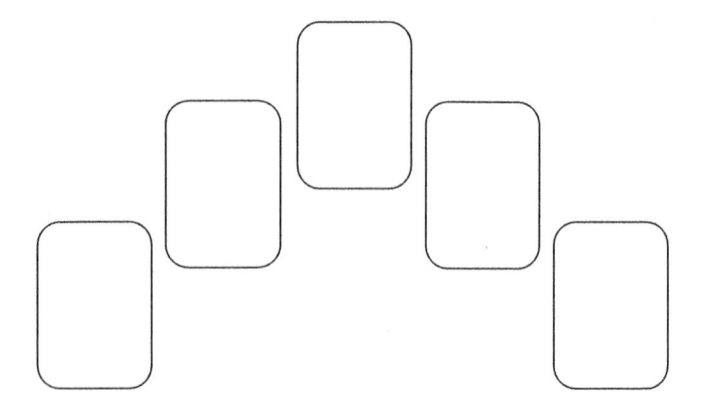

Left – The current situation
Second Left – Your desires
Middle – Something you can't see coming
Second Right – Near future
Right – Future Further Ahead

And Finally...

I hope this book has given you an insight into my journey to becoming a professional tarot reader. I also hope I've managed to enthuse you into picking up a deck and having a go yourself. Being a tarot reader is a really special role and I wouldn't have been able to do it without all the love and support I receive from clients and followers. So thank you for buying this book. I hope you have enjoyed reading it as much as I have enjoyed writing it.

With Love
Becky

To Contact The Author

I would love to hear from you and learn about how this book has helped you.

You can contact me at;
thebeckyclarke@hotmail.com

For more information about me and my services you can head to my website at;
www.thebeckyclarke.co.uk

Or find me on;
Instagram - @thebeckyclarke
Facebook - @thebeckyclarke
TikTok - @the_becky_clarke

Driving our first campervan.

Halloween time.

Secret talents... grade 8 oboe player.

Our first camper out in the snow

Printed in Great Britain
by Amazon